THE LIBRARY OF AMERICAN LIVES AND TIMES™

THOMAS JEFFERSON

Life, Liberty, and the Pursuit of Happiness

Amy Kukla
and
Jon Kukla

The Rosen Publishing Group's
PowerPlus Books™
New York

In memory of
Margaret Sue Copenhaver
Teacher, Librarian, and Friend

Published in 2005 by The Rosen Publishing Group, Inc.
29 East 21st Street, New York, NY 10010

First Edition

Editor's Note: All quotations have been reproduced as they appeared in the letters and diaries from which they were borrowed. No correction was made to the inconsistent spelling that was common in that time period.

Library of Congress Cataloging-in-Publication Data

Kukla, Amy.
Thomas Jefferson : life, liberty, and the pursuit of happiness / Amy Kukla, Jon Kukla.
v. cm. — (The library of American lives and times)
Includes bibliographical references and index.
Contents: Life on the Virginia frontier — Hostility to every form of tyranny — Burgess and patriot — Writing the Declaration of Independence — Laws for the Commonwealth of Virginia — Wartime governor of Virginia — An American in Paris — Secretary of state — Vice president and president — Louisiana for a song — An active retirement.
ISBN 1-4042-2655-9 (lib. bdg.)
1. Jefferson, Thomas, 1743–1826—Juvenile literature. 2. Presidents—United States—Biography—Juvenile literature. [1. Jefferson, Thomas, 1743–1826. 2. Presidents.] I. Kukla, Jon, 1948– II. Title. III. Series.
E332.79 .K85 2005 973.4'6'092—dc22
2003014196

Manufactured in the United States of America

Contents

1. Life on the Virginia Frontier

Wild honeysuckle was beginning to bloom near the Jeffersons' wooden house when Thomas Jefferson was born on April 13, 1743. His parents' house in Virginia overlooked the Rivanna River, a small branch of the James River. Thomas Jefferson's father, Peter, had named their home Shadwell for the parish, or church community, in London, England, where his wife, Jane Randolph, had been baptized. Shadwell was located in the foothills of the Blue Ridge Mountains in an area of Virginia known as the Piedmont.

In the decades before the American Revolution, the Jeffersons and most other Virginians were proud to live in Britain's oldest and largest royal colony in America. The Atlantic Ocean linked Virginians to commerce with Europe. Most Virginians lived on farms or plantations near the James, York, Rappahannock, and Potomac rivers. These great rivers in the Tidewater, or coastal,

---

Opposite: Thomas Jefferson, painted by John Trumbull in 1788, was an open-minded intellectual. Jefferson believed that by examining an idea from different points of view, he would come closer to the truth.

This 1827 watercolor by Jane Pitford Braddick Peticolas depicts a view from the Piedmont region of Virginia. The Piedmont is the hilly area at the base of the Blue Ridge Mountains. On the horizon is the city of Charlottesville, Virginia.

region of Virginia were deep enough for the oceangoing sailing ships of the eighteenth century. Virginians grew food for themselves and raised tobacco that was sold in England and other parts of Europe.

The colony of Virginia was much larger than the state of Virginia is today. When Thomas Jefferson was born, the colony extended west from the Atlantic Ocean all the way to the Mississippi River, and from North Carolina in the south all the way north to the Great Lakes. Virginia was then home to about 180,000 people whose ancestors had emigrated from England, Scotland, and other European countries. The population also included approximately 120,000 enslaved African Americans.

Thomas Jefferson's family had been in the colony since the seventeenth century. His mother's family, the wealthy and prominent Randolphs, had begun to arrive in Virginia from England around 1640, when the colony was young. His great-grandfather on his father's side of the family, who was also named Thomas Jefferson, came from England to America in 1679 and then purchased a tobacco farm along the James River in 1682. By the time his namesake and great-grandson, Thomas, was born in 1743, the Jefferson family was well established.

Although the Jeffersons were prosperous and better educated than most families on smaller farms, they were not as wealthy or prominent as were the aristocratic planters of the Tidewater area. For example, Thomas's wealthy cousins Peyton and John Randolph went abroad to study law in London, an expense that Thomas's parents could not afford.

Thomas's father, Peter Jefferson, was a farmer and a surveyor, but his most famous accomplishment was as a mapmaker. Peter Jefferson and Joshua Fry, his partner and the chief surveyor of Albemarle County, Virginia, drew the Fry-Jefferson map of Virginia that was first published in London in 1751.

This 1755 engraving of Peter Jefferson and Joshua Fry's 1751 map of the Virginia Colony was published in London, England. The color-coded key indicates the locations and borders of New Jersey, Delaware, Pennsylvania, Maryland, Virginia, and North Carolina. Debate over the western boundaries of many of the colonies lasted for decades.

After a few years at Shadwell, Peter Jefferson moved his family to Tuckahoe Plantation, located on the James River about 10 miles (16 km) west of Richmond, Virginia. Tuckahoe had been the home of William and Maria Randolph and their children. After the deaths of William and Maria, who were close friends of the Jeffersons' and Jane Randolph Jefferson's relatives, Peter and Jane Jefferson moved to Tuckahoe to raise the three Randolph children along with their own. This created a large family, as Peter Jefferson and his wife Jane eventually had ten children together, although two of the children died at a young age. Thomas Jefferson was their eldest son.

As a young boy, Thomas Jefferson attended school in this building, which is located on the Tuckahoe Plantation. Jefferson's cousin Thomas Mann Randolph and probably four of Jefferson's sisters, Jane, Mary, Elizabeth, and Martha, attended the school with Jefferson.

Thomas Jefferson attended school in a house on the Tuckahoe Plantation where he learned to read, write, and do arithmetic. After the Randolph children were grown, the Jefferson family moved back to Shadwell.

Peter Jefferson provided well for his family. When he died unexpectedly from unknown causes in the summer of 1757, his estate included sufficient funds for Thomas to carry on his education.

At age nine Thomas Jefferson had begun studying Latin, Greek, and French with a tutor, the Reverend William Douglas. After his father's death when Thomas was fourteen, Thomas Jefferson continued his education and improved his knowledge of languages with another teacher, the Reverend James Maury. The Maury School for Boys was close to Thomas Jefferson's home in Albemarle County, and Jefferson would later describe Maury as "a correct classical scholar." For the rest of his life Jefferson would take pleasure in his ability to read Greek and Roman history and literature in their original languages.

In March 1760, as his seventeenth birthday approached, Jefferson moved to Williamsburg to study at the College of William and Mary. Williamsburg was the capital of Virginia and was located about 120 miles (193 km) east of Shadwell. Jefferson's favorite professor was William Small. Professor Small taught mathematics and natural philosophy, as science was then called, as well as ethics, literature, and rhetoric. "From his conversation," Jefferson wrote, "I got my first views of the expansion of science and of the system of things." Jefferson was a serious student and according to his family he studied about fifteen hours each weekday. He studied past midnight and then woke every morning at six.

Tall, freckled, and sandy-haired, Thomas Jefferson enjoyed the social life of a young Virginian gentleman. He played the violin, rode well on his horse, and had many friends. Jefferson was, however, focused on his personal goals. After graduating from the College of William and Mary in 1762, Jefferson continued to study every day. In addition to reading the great classical writers of Greece and Rome, Jefferson, who thought he might become a lawyer, began to study legal history and law.

John Trumbull sketched George Wythe in Williamsburg, Virginia, on April 25, 1781. In his letters Thomas Jefferson referred to Wythe as "my second father" and "my earliest & best friend."

Professor Small introduced Jefferson to Virginia's British royal governor, Francis Fauquier, and to George Wythe, a respected lawyer and a professor of law who would provide Jefferson with legal instruction. Wythe was the clerk of the House of Burgesses, the colonial legislature. As clerk, Wythe kept the official records of the legislature. Jefferson often visited the House of Burgesses at its yearly meetings in Williamsburg, Virginia.

While still a student, Jefferson frequently dined at the Governor's Palace in Williamsburg. "[Governor Fauquier], Dr. Small and Mr. Wythe . . . and myself, formed a party of four," Jefferson later wrote, "and to the habitual conversations on these occasions I owed much instruction." Governor Fauquier studied science as a hobby. He wrote a report about a Virginian hailstorm that was published by the Royal Society of London, the most important scientific organization in England. The governor also kept a daily record of the weather in Williamsburg and inspired Jefferson to do the same.

When Thomas Jefferson began to study law in 1763, American sentiments toward Britain were changing. The British parliament, which made British laws, had decided to collect taxes from the colonies. This decision was spurred by the huge debt, or money owed, that Britain had acquired while fighting France in the long French and Indian War, fought from 1754 to 1763. In 1765, Parliament passed the Stamp Act, which placed a tax on all printed material in the colonies. Tax stamps were required to be attached to printed materials such as newspapers, legal documents, and playing cards.

Virginians and colonists from other regions opposed the Stamp Act. The colonists had no say in Parliament, because they had no representatives who could speak for them and voice their complaints. The colonists believed that their status as Englishmen gave them the right to decide for themselves through their own officials in America how they should be taxed.

Jefferson was in Williamsburg when the House of Burgesses considered Burgess Patrick Henry's resolutions protesting the Stamp Act in 1765. Jefferson listened to the debate while standing "at the door of the lobby of

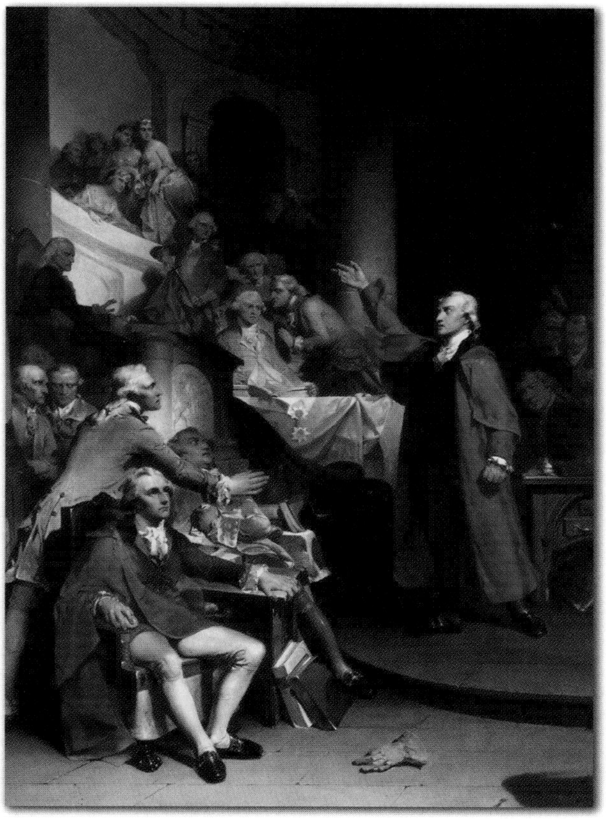

Patrick Henry Before the House of Burgesses, painted by Peter Rothermel in 1851, dramatizes Henry protesting the British Stamp Act. Henry's impassioned speech calling for resistance brought forth several cries of "Treason!" Henry replied, "If this be treason, make the most of it."

the House of Burgesses." Henry proclaimed that Parliament had no authority to tax Virginia's citizens. Jefferson remembered "the splendid display of Mr. Henry's talents as a popular orator. They were great indeed; such as I have never heard from any other man. He appeared to me to speak as Homer wrote." The House of Burgesses voted in favor of Patrick Henry's resolutions.

After passing the required examinations, Jefferson became a lawyer in 1767. For several years he represented clients in the General Court at Williamsburg, the highest court in Virginia.

2. Hostility to Every Form of Tyranny

As a teenager, Thomas Jefferson developed a lifelong interest in religion. The Jeffersons were members of the Church of England, or Anglican Church, which was the established church in colonial Virginia.

PRIERE DE VOLTAIRE.
Ô Dieu qu'on méconnait ; ô Dieu que tout annonce !
Entends les derniers mots que ma bouche prononce.
Si je me suis trompé c'est en cherchant ta Loi,
Mon cœur s'est égaré : mais il est plein de toi ;
Je vois sans m'allarmer l'éternité paraître
Et je ne peux penser qu'un dieu qui m'a fait naître,
Qu'un dieu qui sur mes jours versa tant de bienfaits ;
Quand mes jours sont éteints me tourmente à jamais.

Above is an eighteenth-century engraving of the writer-philosopher Voltaire. In 1764, Voltaire wrote, "Who leads the human race in civilized countries? Those who know how to read and write."

During the seventeenth and eighteenth centuries, Europe and America were experiencing an intellectual movement that was called the Enlightenment. The movement emphasized the importance of science and reason. Before the Enlightenment, religion had been the dominant guiding force in society. Among the Enlightenment's leading thinkers were the French writers Voltaire and Baron de Montesquieu, who

Intellectual movements, such as the Enlightenment, which offer a fresh perspective on the world, gain force by the sharing of ideas through books and conversation. Jefferson's study of Enlightenment philosophers such as John Locke inspired Jefferson's own enlightened thinking and writing in America.

John Locke was a British seventeenth-century philosopher who believed that humans are born equal. Each infant arrives without any knowledge of the world and all that a newborn learns will be acquired through his or her senses. The child of a noble is no better equipped at birth to learn than is the child of a peasant.

Locke also proposed that education for all children, not just those of the nobility, was critical if they were to become moral, productive members of society.

challenged the accuracy of biblical stories and the influence of the Roman Catholic Church in French politics and daily life.

Thomas Jefferson had learned about the ideas of the Enlightenment through his conversations with Governor Fauquier and Professor Small and from his extensive reading of a variety of books and newspapers. Jefferson wanted to make up his own mind about religious truth and not accept ideologies, or beliefs, simply because he was told that they were true. He later wrote, "I have sworn upon the altar of God, eternal hostility against every form of tyranny over the mind of man."

Eventually, after a lifetime of study, Jefferson created his own collection of passages from the Bible for his private meditation, or reflection. Jefferson searched through the Gospels of Matthew, Mark, Luke, and John to find what he felt were the best teachings of Jesus. Jefferson cut out these favored passages from several Bibles, including those written in English, French, Greek, and Latin, and pasted them into a scrapbook that has since become known as the Jefferson Bible.

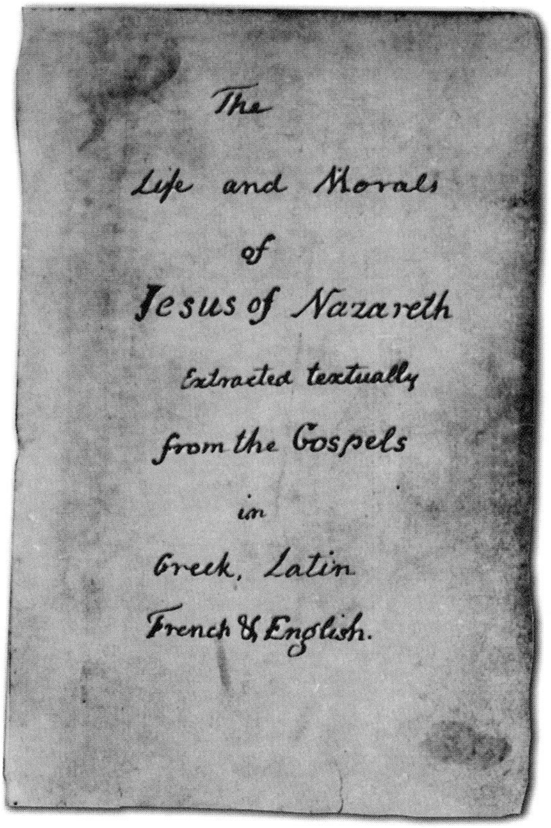

Jefferson handwrote this cover to his personalized collection of biblical passages, which has since become known as the Jefferson Bible.

Jefferson kept the scrapbook to himself. His religious beliefs were his own affair. "Religious opinions," he told a friend, are "a matter between our Maker and ourselves." Throughout Jefferson's political career, many Americans were offended by his attitude toward religion. "I inquire after no man's religion, and trouble none with mine," Jefferson responded. "It is in our lives, and not from our words, that our religion must be read."

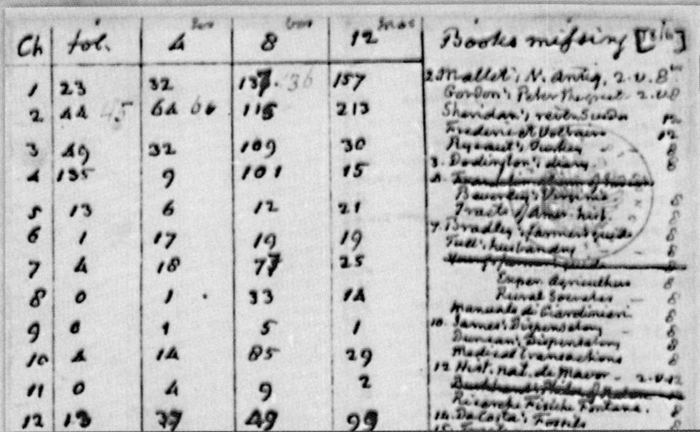

Ch	fol.	4	8	12
1	23	32	137	157
2	44	64	115	213
3	49	32	109	30
4	135	9	101	15
5	13	6	12	21
6	1	17	19	19
7	4	18	77	25
8	0	1	33	14
9	0	1	5	1
10	4	14	85	29
11	0	4	9	2
12	13	37	49	99

This is a section of the catalog that Thomas Jefferson drew up around March 1815, in preparation for his sale of 6,487 books to Congress in 1815. Jefferson tried to organize his book collection by subject and chronology.

Thomas Jefferson loved to read and first began buying books in college. During his lifetime he gathered books for three private libraries. The first of his libraries consisted mostly of law books and classics. These books burned along with the house at Shadwell in 1770. Within one decade Jefferson's second library amounted to about 2,640 volumes.

Jefferson called his second library "the choicest collection of books in the United States." In 1815, Jefferson sold 6,487 volumes to the United States to restore the Library of Congress collection, which had burned when the British invaded Washington, D.C., during the War of 1812.

As soon as Jefferson shipped these books to Washington, he began collecting more books. By the time of his death Jefferson's third library, once again heavy in classics, numbered several thousand volumes.

The strict study habits that Thomas Jefferson developed in college shaped his behavior as an adult. He kept a clock on the wall above his bed and rose early. Every morning he read from religious or classical literature before starting the day's business. Almost every day he wrote letters to his friends and colleagues throughout the world. Eventually, the total number of letters that Jefferson wrote in his lifetime would amount to about nineteen thousand. In addition to his language studies, Jefferson also recorded the weather conditions. For the last fifty years of his life, he took the outside temperature nearly every morning at dawn and then again every afternoon at about three o'clock.

Once Jefferson had established his law practice, he took time from his daily routine to socialize. Thomas Jefferson met Martha Wayles Skelton, a young widow, in the autumn of 1770.

Martha had moved back into her parents' house in Charles City County, near Williamsburg, Virginia, after her first husband, Bathurst Skelton, had died. The couple had one son, John, who died around the age of four. Martha's mother, Martha Eppes Wayles, had died soon after Martha's birth. Martha's father, John Wayles, had remarried two more times after his first wife's death.

Martha was a talented musician who could play the pianoforte and the harpsichord. One of Jefferson's

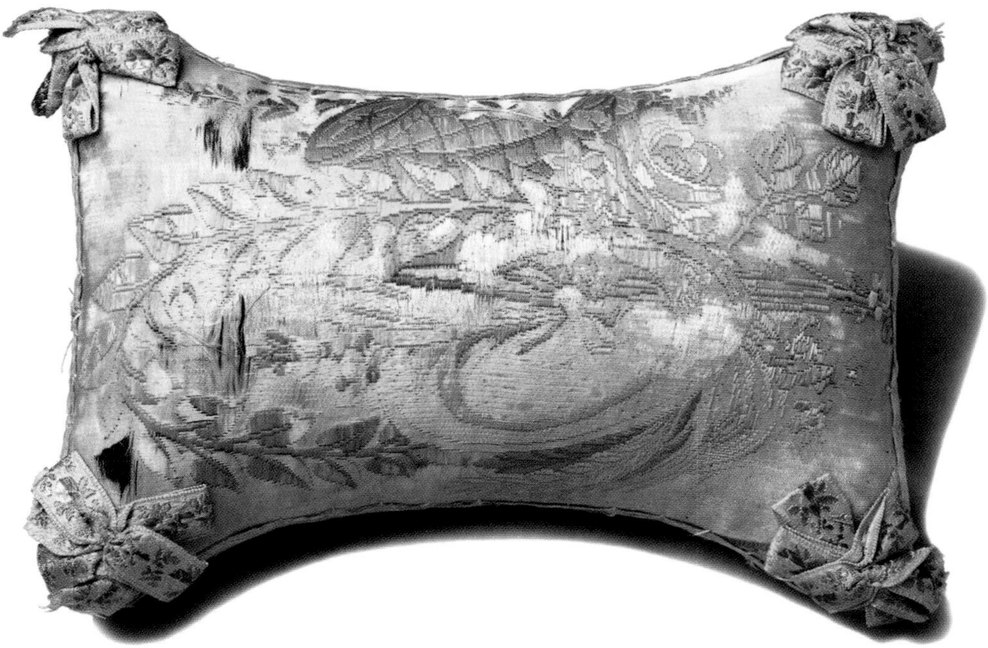

Martha Wayles Skelton Jefferson did the delicate needlework on this pincushion sometime between 1772 and 1782.

first gifts to her was a pianoforte, an instrument that is similar to a piano. Martha was lovely and good-natured, and she had several suitors competing for her attention.

On a New Year's Day in 1772, twenty-nine-year-old Thomas Jefferson married twenty-four-year-old Martha Wayles Skelton. After their wedding Thomas and Martha moved into Jefferson's unfinished house called Monticello, located a few miles (km) west of the ruins of Shadwell, which had burned down in 1770. Jefferson owned about 10,000 acres (4,046.9 ha) of land at Monticello and Shadwell and between 100 and 200 slaves. His total holdings of property included land and slaves that he had inherited from his father, land and slaves that Martha had inherited from her father, and some additional property that Jefferson had purchased on his own.

Monticello, which means "little mountain" in Italian, was built on a mountain on a prime piece of property that overlooked the town of Charlottesville. Jefferson designed the house himself and was always "putting up

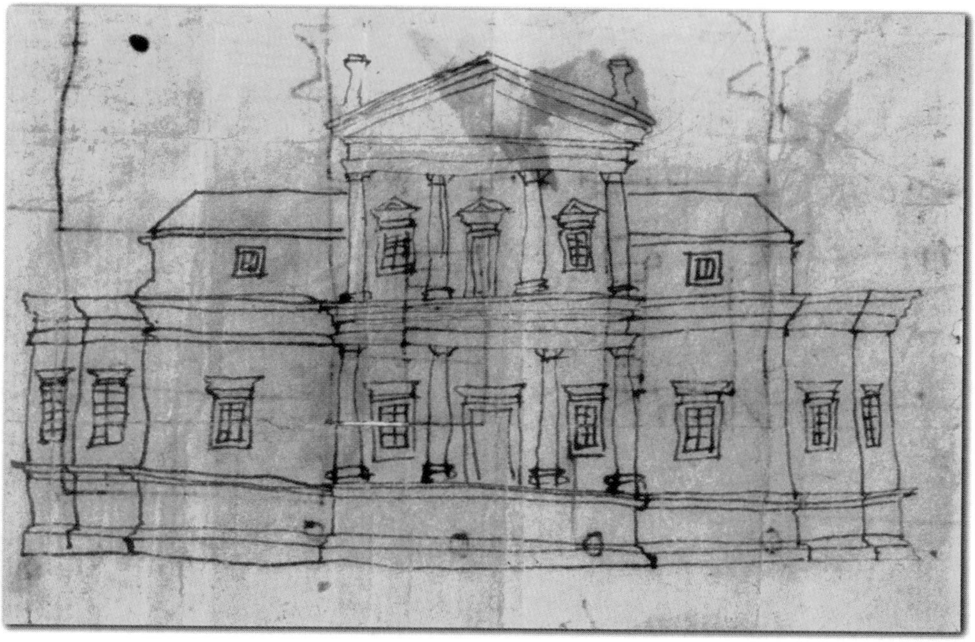

Thomas Jefferson created this drawing of Monticello around 1770. A passion for nature influenced Jefferson's choice in building Monticello far from a city. Jefferson believed that people who lived in the country and worked the land were both physically healthier and morally fitter than people who spent their lives in cities.

and pulling down" parts of it. He started the first plans for Monticello in 1767 and continued to make changes on the house until he died. "Architecture is my delight," he told visitors.

During the ten years that Thomas and Martha Jefferson were married, they had six children. Three died in infancy, and another daughter died when she was two. Only their eldest daughter Martha, nicknamed Patsy, and her sister Maria, nicknamed Polly, lived to adulthood.

3. Burgess and Patriot

Since the founding of a colony in 1607, on an island the settlers called Jamestown, Virginians had lived under English law. The king and his advisers sent a representative from England to be the colony's royal governor. The king also appointed important colonial planters to the Council of Virginia. These members of the Council, or councillors, shared executive power with the governor and advised him about making laws and choosing officials for the county courts and militia. The councillors also served as the General Court, Virginia's highest judicial body.

The citizens of each county in Virginia, however, elected their own lawmakers, called burgesses. Virginia's government was fashioned after the English parliament, which had an upper house called the House of Lords and a lower house called the House of Commons. The lords were aristocrats who inherited their positions. The commons were elected by the people. In Virginia, the Council served as the upper house of the General Assembly, while the House of Burgesses was the lower house. The burgesses met in Williamsburg, where they passed laws for the colony and decided what taxes would be collected.

After working for two years as a lawyer, Thomas Jefferson entered politics in December 1768, after the voters of Albemarle County elected him to the House of Burgesses. In 1770, he was also named county lieutenant, the officer in command of Albemarle County's volunteer militia, an army composed of volunteers. Jefferson would serve in the Virginia legislature until 1775.

Unlike his friend Patrick Henry, Jefferson was not an effective public speaker. As a member of the House of Burgesses, Thomas Jefferson did most of his legislative work in committees, where his skill as a writer was

The Governor's Palace in Williamsburg, Virginia, was rebuilt in 1930. A 1781 fire destroyed the original building. The reconstruction was based on eighteenth-century engravings and artifacts, including a drawing of the mansion done by Thomas Jefferson. The Governor's Palace was erected to serve as the residence of Virginia's British royal governor.

valued. Politicians, Jefferson thought, spent "too much [time] talking, [but] how can it be otherwise in a body to which the people send 150 lawyers, whose trade it is to question everything, yield nothing & talk by the hour?"

Although Britain had repealed the detested Stamp Act in 1766, Parliament still insisted that it could pass laws for and impose taxes on the American colonies. Virginians disagreed that Parliament had the right to pass laws or impose taxes without first obtaining the approval of the colonial legislature. After Parliament repealed the Stamp Act, they replaced it with the Declaratory Act. This law stated that Parliament had power over the colonies in all matters, including the right to tax them. The situation remained tense for several years and then became still more strained when Parliament ordered a tax to be placed on tea.

In December 1773, a group of patriots disguised as Native Americans threw a cargo of British East India Company tea into Boston Harbor, rather than allow the tea to be sold in America and the tax collected. Parliament sent British troops to oversee the punishment of the city of Boston, to close its port, and to force the colonists to submit to parliamentary authority.

When the news from Boston reached Virginia, some of the younger burgesses agreed "that we must boldly take [a] stand in the line with Massachusetts." Patrick Henry, Richard Henry Lee, Thomas Jefferson, and a few others met together in the council chamber. These Virginians wanted to support the patriots in Boston by boycotting, or refusing to purchase, anything imported from Britain.

The best way to bring all the burgesses together in support of a boycott, they thought, was to hold a prayer meeting at Bruton Parish Church in Williamsburg, Virginia. On May 24, after consulting some old books about Parliament and English law, Jefferson later recalled, "we cooked up a resolution, somewhat modernizing their phrases, for appointing the 1st day of June . . . a day of fasting, humiliation and prayer."

To win supporters for the June 1 prayer meeting, Jefferson and his friends asked Robert Carter Nicholas,

The watercolor of Bruton Parish Church in Williamsburg, Virginia, was done by Francis Dayton in 1950. The artist based his depiction of the colonial church on an earlier work done by Sidney King.

"whose grave & religious character was more in unison with the tone of our resolution," to introduce their plan to the House of Burgesses. "He moved it the same day," Jefferson wrote, "and it passed without opposition."

The royal governor, after learning the purpose of the planned prayer meeting, sent a message to the burgesses on May 26 telling them to dissolve, or end, their session and to go home. According to British law, once the session was dissolved the men were no longer burgesses and had no right to conduct business for the colony. However, instead of going home, the former burgesses walked down the street to Raleigh Tavern, which had the largest private meeting room in Williamsburg. There, on May 27, the former burgesses agreed to a boycott of imported goods from Britain.

At Raleigh Tavern, the Virginians formed a committee of correspondence to work with similar committees that were being formed in the other thirteen colonies. These committees worked together to organize and communicate details of their rebellion against British tyranny.

The June 1, 1774, day of fasting and prayer for American freedom was a success and Jefferson wrote that it "was like a shock of electricity." The Virginians prayed for "heaven to avert from us the evils of civil war, to inspire us with firmness in support of our rights, and to turn the hearts of the King and parliament to moderation and justice."

4. Writing the Declaration of Independence

On August 1, 1774, a group of Virginians elected by each county gathered in Williamsburg for a special convention that was organized to protect their rights and to encourage unity with the other thirteen colonies. Thomas Jefferson fell ill on his way to the Virginia convention. Therefore, he sent copies of his long pamphlet on American rights to the convention by messenger, where it was read aloud.

Published in 1774 with the title *A Summary View of the Rights of British America*, Jefferson's booklet stated that Parliament had no authority over the American colonies. "Kings," he wrote, "are the servants, not the proprietors of the people." Americans could not be taxed "by any power on earth but our own," he wrote. "The God who gave us life, gave us liberty at the same time." Jefferson hoped that King George III would "quiet the minds of [his] subjects in British America" by respecting American liberty.

The Virginia convention of 1774 also sent George Washington and other Virginian leaders to Philadelphia,

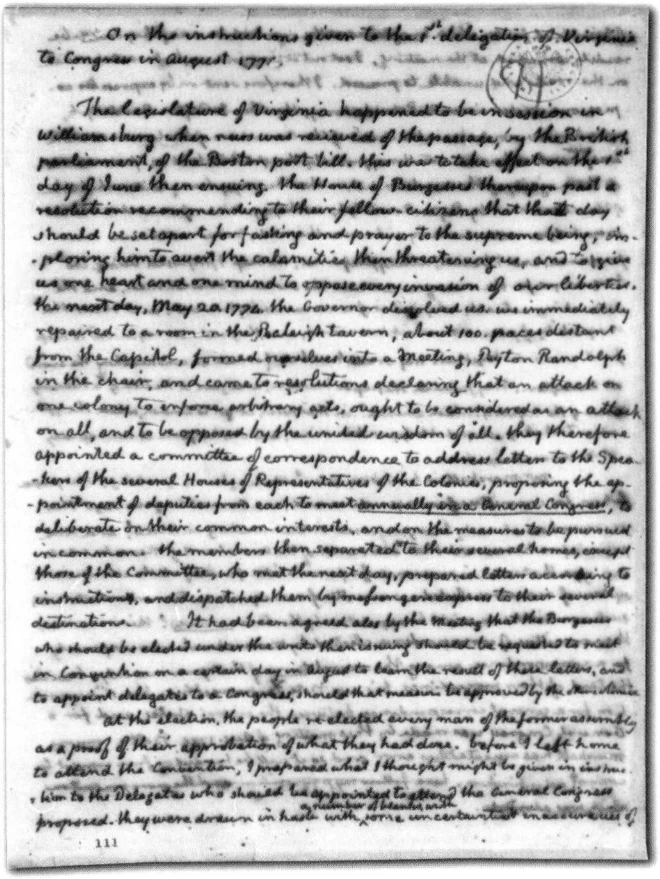

On the instructions given to the 1st. delegation of Virginia to Congress in August 1774.

The legislature of Virginia happened to be in session in Williamsburg when news was recieved of the passage, by the British parliament, of the Boston port bill. this was to take effect on the 1st. day of June then ensuing. the House of Burgesses thereupon past a resolution recommending to their fellow-citizens that that day should be set apart for fasting and prayer to the supreme being, imploring him to avert the calamities then threatening us, and to give us one heart and one mind to oppose every invasion of our liberties. the next day, May 20. 1774. the Governor dissolved us. we immediately repaired to a room in the Raleigh tavern, about 100. paces distant from the Capitol, formed ourselves into a meeting, Peyton Randolph in the chair, and came to resolutions declaring that an attack on one colony to enforce arbitrary acts, ought to be considered as an attack on all, and to be opposed by the united wisdom of all. they therefore appointed a committee of correspondence to address letters to the Speakers of the several Houses of Representatives of the Colonies, proposing the appointment of deputies from each to meet annually in a General Congress, to deliberate on their common interests, and on the measures to be pursued in common. the members then separated to their several homes, except those of the Committee, who met the next day, prepared letters according to instructions, and dispatched them by messengers express to their several destinations. It had been agreed also by the Meeting that the Burgesses who should be elected under the writs then issuing should be requested to meet in Convention on a certain day in August to learn the result of these letters, and to appoint delegates to a Congress, should that measure be approved by the other colonies. At the election, the people re-elected every man of the former assembly as a proof of their approbation of what they had done. before I left home to attend the Convention, I prepared what I thought might be given in instruction to the Delegates who should be appointed to attend the General Congress proposed. they were drawn in haste with a number of blanks with some uncertainties and inaccuracies of

111

Thomas Jefferson wrote this draft of his booklet *A Summary View of the Rights of British America* in August 1774. Jefferson's complaints against King George III would be labeled treason, an offense that was punishable by hanging.

Pennsylvania, for the First Continental Congress, held that same autumn. During this meeting the Continental Congress took important steps toward independence. The colonies developed a nonimportation association that put pressure on British merchants by refusing to import British goods. The delegates to the

First Continental Congress hoped their boycott would force Parliament to stop taxing the colonists without first obtaining their consent. Thomas Jefferson was sent to the next Congress in 1775, when Peyton Randolph, the leader of Virginia's delegation, had to return to his home in Williamsburg.

At the Second Continental Congress many delegates were still reluctant to speak of separation from Britain. The delegates from New York and Pennsylvania hoped that, if Parliament stopped threatening the rights of the colonists, America could remain within the British Empire. However, on April 19, 1775, events moved the colonies toward war with Britain. At Lexington and Concord, west of Boston, Massachusetts, American militia and British soldiers had exchanged gunfire.

Jefferson left for Albemarle County, Virginia, in December 1775 to spend time at home with his family. Also, Virginia wanted him to serve as commander of the Albemarle County militia. As commander, Jefferson drew up lists of the militia volunteers and their assigned duties. He was responsible for supervising the militia's training through ongoing drills and for maintaining the number of volunteers at a satisfactory level. Additionally, Jefferson headed military courts-martial, or trials for members of the armed forces.

While he was at Monticello, Jefferson's mother, Jane, died from a stroke at Shadwell on March 31, 1776. Thomas Jefferson did not write much about his feelings for his mother, either while she was living or after her death.

Jefferson returned to Philadelphia in May to aid Congress. On June 7, 1776, Richard Henry Lee, the leader of Virginia's delegation to Congress, presented a resolution for independence from Britain. During June, the delegates from each colony debated whether to vote for or against independence. Congress asked Jefferson and four other delegates to write down America's reasons for seeking independence from Britain. The four other delegates included John Adams from Massachusetts, Benjamin Franklin from Pennsylvania, Robert R. Livingston from New York, and Roger Sherman from Connecticut. Thomas Jefferson, however, was the delegate who did most of the writing.

Thomas Jefferson and the others finished their work at the end of June. They gave copies of the Declaration of Independence to all the members of Congress on June 28. The document had three major parts.

The first part of the Declaration of Independence, called the preamble, states that Americans believe "all men are created equal." It goes on to describe how everyone has rights that cannot be taken away, and "that among these are Life, Liberty, and the pursuit of

Next page: This is Thomas Jefferson's 1776 draft of the Declaration of Independence. Congress deleted passages from Jefferson's draft, including sentences that spoke of sorrow for the colonies' separation from Britain: "We might have been a free & great people together."

A Declaration by the Representatives of the UNITED STATES OF AMERICA, in General Congress assembled.

When in the course of human events it becomes necessary for one people to dissolve the political bands which have connected them with another, and to assume among the powers of the earth the separate and equal station to which the laws of nature & of nature's god entitle them, a decent respect to the opinions of mankind requires that they should declare the causes which impel them to the separation.

We hold these truths to be self-evident; that all men are created equal; that they are endowed by their creator with [inherent & inalienable] rights; that among these are life, liberty, & the pursuit of happiness; that to secure these rights, governments are instituted among men, deriving their just powers from the consent of the governed; that whenever any form of government becomes destructive of these ends, it is the right of the people to alter or to abolish it, & to institute new government, laying it's foundation on such principles & organising it's powers in such form, as to them shall seem most likely to effect their safety & happiness. prudence indeed will dictate that governments long established should not be changed for light & transient causes: and accordingly all experience hath shewn that mankind are more disposed to suffer while evils are sufferable, than to right themselves by abolishing the forms to which they are accustomed. but when a long train of abuses & usurpations [begun at a distinguished period, &] pursuing invariably the same object, evinces a design to reduce them under absolute Despotism, it is their right, it is their duty, to throw off such government & to provide new guards for their future security. such has been the patient sufferance of these colonies; & such is now the necessity which constrains them to [expunge] their former systems of government. the history of the present king of Great Britain is a history of [unremitting] injuries and usurpations, [among which, appears no solitary fact to contradict the uniform tenor of the rest, all of which have] in direct object the establishment of an absolute tyranny over these states. to prove this, let facts be submitted to a candid world, [for the truth of which we pledge a faith yet unsullied by falsehood]

Dr. Franklin's hand

Mr. Adams's hand

Happiness." When governments are formed, they should obtain their power from the consent of the people, and not from the will of a king. If a government does wrong, the people have a right "to alter or to abolish it, and . . . [create a] new Government." It is not wise to change governments over little things. If a government becomes a tyranny, however, the people can and should replace it with a better one. "[I]t is their right, it is their duty," to protect liberty for themselves and future generations. Congress did not make many changes to the first part of Jefferson's declaration.

This 1855 photograph of the corner of Seventh and Market Streets in Philadelphia shows the building where Jefferson drafted the Declaration of Independence. Jefferson rented the second floor from the building's owner, Jacob Graff.

The second part listed the many terrible things that King George III had done to the colonists. "The history of the present King of Great Britain," the declaration said, "is a history of repeated injuries and usurpations. . . ." Jefferson listed more than twenty acts of tyranny by

André Basset l'aîné, who created this image in Paris in the 1770s, depicted Continental soldiers pulling down the statue of King George III on July 9, 1776. The event took place on Broadway at Bowling Green, which is located near the southernmost tip of Manhattan, New York. The colonists later melted the metal statue to create 42,088 bullets for the Continental army.

George III. One abuse in the list was that King George III had placed "taxes on us without our consent." The members of Congress discussed these statements carefully and made a number of changes to the second section. They removed Jefferson's criticism of the slave trade when the delegates from the states of Georgia and South Carolina protested its inclusion in the document.

The third section was the conclusion. It included all the words of the resolution for independence presented by Richard Henry Lee, which Congress had passed on

July 2. This final section announced the name of the new country: the United States of America. The conclusion stated that this newly independent nation could make war, negotiate treaties, and "do all other Acts and Things which independent states may of right do." In its final sentence, the members of Congress promised to uphold this Declaration of Independence with their lives, their wealth, and their "sacred Honor."

Once the changes were made, Congress voted to adopt the Declaration of Independence on July 4, 1776. John Hancock, the president of Congress, witnessed the document, or made it official, by signing it.

Copies of the document were published and read in cities and towns throughout America.

On July 19, 1776, Congress voted "that the Declaration passed on the 4th [should] be fairly engrossed on parchment . . . [and then] be signed by every member of Congress." Important colonial laws were recorded

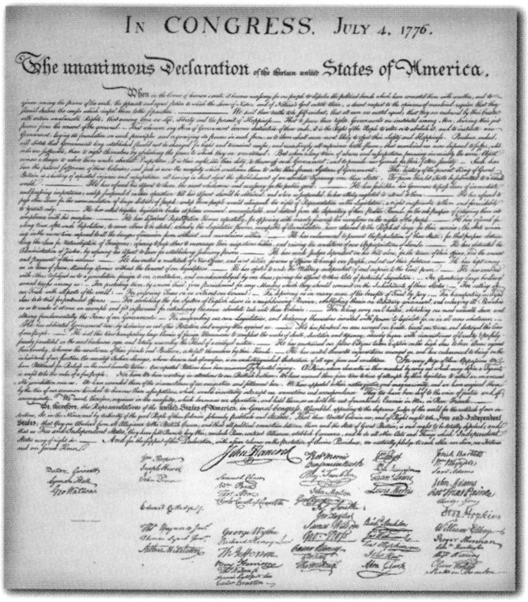

IN CONGRESS. JULY 4, 1776.

The unanimous Declaration of the ... States of America,

This copy of the Declaration of Independence was made from an 1823 engraving done by William J. Stone. The original 1776 document is housed in the Rotunda of the National Archives Building in Washington, D.C.

on parchment, a material made from animal skins that was especially durable. A clerk took a fine quill pen and copied the entire Declaration of Independence onto a large sheet of very thin leather. The task took the clerk more than one week. When he finished his work, on August 2, most of the members of Congress signed the Declaration of Independence. A few men who were absent signed it later.

The United States claimed to be an independent nation. If America's war against Britain failed, the men who had signed the Declaration of Independence risked being captured by the British and then executed as traitors.

5. Laws for the Commonwealth of Virginia

In September 1776, Thomas Jefferson left Congress and returned to Virginia. During Jefferson's absence, Virginia's royal governor had fled from Williamsburg after angry patriots demanded the return of gunpowder that had been seized by British royal forces from the public arsenal, or storehouse of weapons, in Williamsburg. The British feared that the patriots would use the gunpowder against them. The Virginia colony had declared itself to be an independent state in June 1776, and had chosen Patrick Henry as its first governor.

George Mason was the primary author of the Virginia Constitution of 1776. This document created the Commonwealth of Virginia. Although Jefferson had also drafted a version of Virginia's constitution, only his preamble was kept in the final document. Virginia's new constitution

Thomas Jefferson considered George Mason, painted by Dominic Boudet, "a man of the first order of wisdom. . . ."

had two major parts. One section set up the government. The other section was the Declaration of Rights, which was written by George Mason and Patrick Henry with the intention of protecting the liberties of the people.

Virginia's constitution changed the House of Burgesses into the House of Delegates and established a senate instead of a colonial council. The governor was to be elected by the legislature for a term of one year. Governors could be reelected twice for a total of three consecutive years in office. They had much less power over the people of Virginia than the royal governors of the colony had once held.

Jefferson became a member of the House of Delegates in October 1776. Although Jefferson admired the Virginia Declaration of Rights, he also believed that independence gave Virginians a chance to reform certain existing statutes that he thought were old-fashioned or unfair. A statute is a law that has been passed by the legislative body of a government.

Between 1776 and 1779, Jefferson worked hard to revise the laws of Virginia. Along with his former law professor, George Wythe, and the important judge Edmund Pendleton, Jefferson served on a small but powerful committee that drafted 126 new laws for the Commonwealth of Virginia. The committee submitted its proposals to the legislature in June 1779.

One of these laws initiated a change in the way families passed their lands from generation to generation.

This 1794 depiction of the Great Seal of Virginia was created by Amos Doolittle. The seal was one of fourteen interlocking seals, one for each of the original thirteen states, plus the seal of the United States, which surrounded a portrait of President George Washington.

"Commonwealth" is an English word that is similar in meaning to the Latin phrase res publica, *which means "for the common good" or "for the good of the public."*

The word "republic" also comes from the phrase res publica. *A republic is a government without a king, where power resides with the people.*

Today the states of Virginia, Massachusetts, Pennsylvania, and Kentucky are still officially known as commonwealths.

When Virginia was a British colony, only the eldest son could inherit his family plantation after his father had died. Younger children received nothing. This English law, called primogeniture, prevented large plantations from being divided into smaller ones. Primogeniture supported aristocracy, or rule by the few, because the eldest son would have wealth, power, and an important place in society. Jefferson wrote a law against primogeniture so that children would share their family's inheritance more equally. Smaller independent farms, he thought, would promote liberty and self-government in Virginia. The legislature passed Jefferson's land reform law in 1785.

Jefferson also sought to reform public education. Wealthy planters could hire private tutors for their children. They could send their boys to the College of William and Mary in Williamsburg. Sometimes they sent their sons to colleges such as Princeton and Harvard, or even to British universities across the Atlantic Ocean. Less wealthy farmers could sometimes find schools run by Anglican ministers for their children. Occasionally, small farmers could also afford to send their boys to William and Mary. No schooling was available for poor people or slaves, however. Formal education for girls was limited, too, although some wealthy families hired tutors for their daughters.

Jefferson and his committee drafted laws to create a complete system of public education. His plan included public elementary schools, middle schools, high schools,

Construction on the College of William and Mary began in 1695. Initially, the building shown above housed the entire college. The British architect Sir Christopher Wren is believed to have designed the structure. This painting was created in the early 1900s.

and a new state university. The legislature refused to adopt this expensive plan. Without support for education in the House of Delegates, Jefferson's additional efforts to create a public library failed as well.

A proposed law to ensure freedom of religion was another important part of Jefferson's work in the legislature. However, six years would pass before the legislature adopted his bill for religious liberty. James Madison would finally steer the bill to adoption in January 1786, while Jefferson was in Paris. The Virginia Statute for Religious Freedom became the first

American law ever enacted to provide not only for religious toleration but also for the complete freedom of conscience. Freedom of conscience encouraged citizens to practice the religion of their choice.

The eloquent language of Jefferson's Statute for Religious Freedom makes it one of the great statements of American freedom. "Almighty God hath created the mind free," Jefferson wrote. "All attempts to influence it by . . . punishments . . . tend only to beget habits of hypocrisy and meanness." Forcing people to support a church with their taxes was wrong, Jefferson believed.

Jefferson thought that making people attend or join any specific church in order to hold public office was also wrong. "Our civil rights have no dependence upon our religious opinions," the statute proclaimed, "any more than our opinions in physics or geometry." The statute declared that although the Creator controlled both the body and the mind, the Creator did not force people to join any church. Along with George Mason and Patrick Henry's Declaration of Rights, Jefferson's Statute for Religious Freedom remains law in the Commonwealth of Virginia to this day.

6. Wartime Governor of Virginia

Thomas Jefferson labored hard to reform Virginia's laws between 1776 and 1779. On June 1, 1779, the legislature of Virginia showed their respect for Jefferson by electing him as governor. Although Jefferson was reelected the next year, he discovered that his powers as governor were few. The governor could not veto legislation and his own proposed laws had to be approved by the eight-man Council of State that was elected by the legislature as well. When this council made decisions, the governor could only cast a vote in the event of a tie. By the autumn of his second term, Governor Jefferson had grown tired of the office and was eager for his term to end.

While Thomas Jefferson was governor, the American Revolution continued to be fought. The British, however, had shifted their attack from New England to the southern states. Early in January 1781, British troops led by General Benedict Arnold, an American general who had defected to the enemy, conducted a surprise raid on Richmond, Virginia, which had become the state's capital in 1780. Although Jefferson was warned that a British

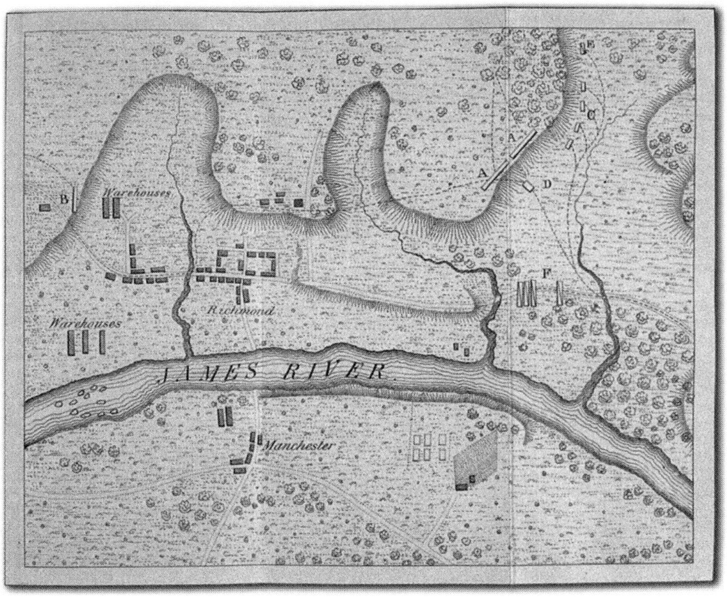

This map was contained in Lieutenant-Colonel John Graves Simcoe's Revolutionary War journal, first published around 1784. Simcoe commanded a corps of Queen's Rangers, a loyalist military corps that fought for Britain. This map details the Queen's Rangers' position before the planned attack on Richmond, Virginia, in January 1781.

fleet was advancing on Richmond, he hesitated before calling out the militia. When he did give the order on January 2, it was too late to fend off the invasion. Benedict Arnold's troops burned a few buildings and then left. Angry critics accused Jefferson of poor leadership during a time of crisis, despite his efforts to protect the buildings and property of the state. That same spring British general Charles Cornwallis and the main British army moved north into Virginia from North Carolina. As the large army advanced toward the capital, the governor and the legislature were forced to flee from Richmond to

Charlottesville, about 80 miles (128.7 km) west in the foothills of the Blue Ridge Mountains.

Thomas Jefferson's second term as governor was almost at an end. The election of a new governor was scheduled for June 4, 1781. The morning of the intended election, however, Lieutenant Colonel Banastre Tarleton ordered a company of British cavalry to race toward Charlottesville. The cavalry, under the command of Captain McLeod, hoped to surprise the governor and the

Governor Jefferson had problems raising money to outfit the Virginians who served in the Continental army. Although he obtained funds by selling the property of British subjects who had lived in Virginia, the money did not go far because of wartime inflation and a drop in the value of Virginia's currency. Mather Brown painted Jefferson in 1786.

legislature and capture them. Luckily, a Virginian horseman named Jack Jouett saw the British pass by the Cuckoo Tavern in Louisa, Virginia, on the night of June 3. Jouett rode about 40 miles (64.4 km) to Monticello and warned Jefferson of the British cavalry's approach.

The legislators met quickly and voted to adjourn, or end the session, and then to cross the Blue Ridge Mountains to Staunton, Virginia. Jefferson sent his family to the Blenheim Plantation, south of Monticello in Albemarle County, where they would be safe. Jefferson devoted most of June 4 to loading papers and documents onto wagons so that they could be carried to safety.

When at last Jefferson saw through his telescope that British troops were approaching Monticello, he mounted his horse, rode into the woods south of his house, and rejoined his family. Later he moved his wife and children and the governor's official papers to Poplar Forest, his plantation retreat, a quiet relaxing place located about 93 miles (149.7 km) to the south in Bedford County.

When the legislators were finally able to assemble in Staunton, they elected General Thomas Nelson as the next governor. Nelson was the highest-ranking officer in the state militia. As the new wartime governor, Nelson was accorded both civilian and military authority sufficient to deal with the invasion. Immediately after electing Jefferson's successor, the legislature called for an investigation into Governor Jefferson's handling of the emergency created by Arnold's and Tarleton's raids.

During this investigation, British luck changed for the worse during the summer of 1781. The French had joined the Americans in their fight against Britain the previous year. The combined Continental and French army and the French navy forced General Cornwallis to surrender at Yorktown, Virginia, in October 1781. The defeat ended the war for independence, although the official treaty was not signed in Paris until 1783.

With the danger of attack past, the Virginian legislature declared that Jefferson, in fact, had done nothing wrong during the British raids. The lawmakers expressed their "high opinion of Mr. Jefferson's ability." They voted and then gave their unanimous, or total, appreciation for his leadership.

Despite these words of praise, the inquiry had angered Jefferson. He had devoted twelve years to public service and considered the legislative inquiry an insult. On the same day that the legislature voted to praise his conduct as governor, Virginia's lawmakers also elected Jefferson as a delegate to Congress. Jefferson said no to the post. He was disgusted with politics. "I am fond of quiet," Jefferson wrote in 1785 to his friend Abigail Adams, whose husband, John Adams, had helped Jefferson to write the Declaration of Independence.

Jefferson told a friend that the legislature's treatment of him "was a shock." The lawmakers had been present during both emergencies and should have known that Jefferson had done all that he could do. He told his friend James Monroe, "These injuries . . . inflicted a wound on my spirit which will only be cured by the all-healing grave."

Sadly, greater sorrow soon followed. Medicine was primitive in Jefferson's day, and childbirth was much more dangerous than it is today. "Mrs. Jefferson has added another daughter to our family," Jefferson wrote to James Monroe on May 20, 1782. However, Martha Wayles Jefferson had not regained her strength after the birth of Lucy Elizabeth on May 8. Martha "still continues very dangerously ill," Jefferson wrote.

This 1789 miniature of Jefferson's daughter Martha "Patsy" Jefferson was painted by Joseph Boze in Paris. Miniatures such as this one were sometimes worn as pendants or bracelets.

Never far from her room, Jefferson watched over his wife all summer. "When not at her bedside," his eldest daughter, Martha, wrote, "he was writing in a small room which opened immediately at the head of her bed." Only ten months after Thomas Jefferson's shock over the legislative inquiry, Martha Wayles Jefferson died on September 6, 1782. Thomas Jefferson, his daughter wrote, "was led from the room . . . into his library where he fainted and remained so long insensible that they feared he never would revive." Jefferson stayed in his room for three weeks, pacing the floor night and day. "When at last he left his room," a friend reported, Jefferson spent his days "on horseback rambling about the mountain."

As winter approached, Jefferson's daughters witnessed "many a violent burst of grief" from their father. Then finally, in November 1782, a messenger arrived with a letter from Philadelphia. Congress wanted to send Jefferson abroad to Paris as a peace commissioner to help the United States negotiate the treaty with Britain and France that would officially end the American Revolution. Jefferson's friends hoped the job might lure him back into public life and ease his grief.

About ten weeks after Martha's death, Jefferson said he began recovering from "a stupor of mind which had rendered me . . . dead to the world. . . ." Jefferson hoped that he might escape his sorrow and his disappointment with Virginian politics by accepting the position. Though he was ready to return to work, Jefferson would never completely get over his grief.

Although it was common for people to marry again after the loss of a spouse, during her illness Martha had asked Jefferson never to remarry. She hoped to ensure that her daughters would grow up happier than she had with her two stepmothers. Jefferson kept his promise.

7. An American in Paris

Thomas Jefferson's departure for France was delayed until July 1784, but Jefferson kept busy in the meantime. He was elected to Congress in spring 1783. In the fall of that year, Jefferson spent six months in Philadelphia developing Congress's plans for the new nation. These plans included the design of America's monetary system.

America's money at the time consisted only of coins. The dollar, which was then a coin, was named for the Spanish dollar. The Spanish dollar also went by the name "piece of eight," because the coin was frequently divided into eight smaller pieces. Jefferson chose to divide the U.S. dollar into tenths to create the dime, which was originally spelled "disme," and then again into hundredths to create the penny. His choice of dividing the dollar into tenths was deliberate. Jefferson thought that using tenths would make it easier for Americans to multiply and divide when using money.

Jefferson also encouraged Virginia to give up its land claims north and west of the Ohio River. Several states

When the United States began minting coins using a monetary system based on decimals, or tenths, a decision was made to start with coins of lesser value. These coins required less metal to produce. Therefore, the silver half disme, whose modern equivalent is the U.S. nickel, was created in 1792. Shown are both sides of the half disme.

held competing claims to land west of the Appalachian Mountains. By surrendering its land claim, Virginia encouraged other states to do the same and thereby promoted more friendly relations amongst all the states. Although the Commonwealth of Virginia would still include present-day Kentucky and West Virginia, the rest of the land became the property of the United States.

Jefferson then started to plan how the land west of the Appalachian Mountains would be divided into new states. Congress later adopted many of these ideas into the framework of the proposed Northwest Ordinance.

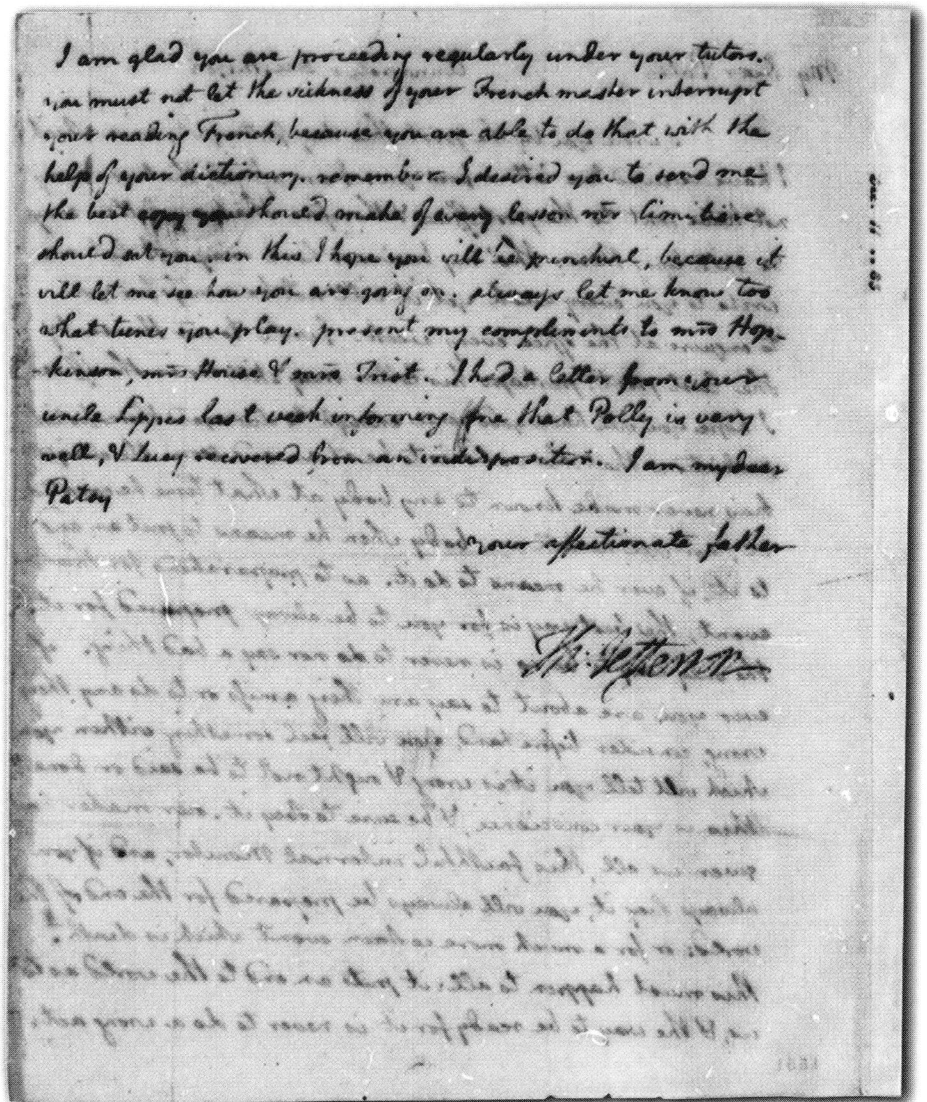

I am glad you are proceeding regularly under your tutors. You must not let the sickness of your French master interrupt your reading French, because you are able to do that with the help of your dictionary. remember I desired you to send me the best copy you should make of every lesson mr Cimitiere should set you. in this I hope you will be punctual, because it will let me see how you are going on. always let me know too what tunes you play. present my compliments to mrs Hopkinson, mrs House & mrs Trist. I had a letter from your uncle Eppes last week informing me that Polly is very well, & Lucy recovered from an indisposition. I am my dear Patsy

your affectionate father

Th: Jefferson

Thomas Jefferson wrote to his daughter Martha, nicknamed Patsy, on December 11, 1783. Jefferson, who had left his daughter in the care of Mrs. Thomas Hopkinson in Philadelphia, kept abreast of his children's education and wrote, "You must not let the sickness of your French master interrupt your reading French, because you are able to do that with the help of your dictionary."

The Northwest Ordinance of 1787 said that public land should be divided into 6-mile (9.7-km) squares called townships, and 1-mile (1.6-km) squares called sections. Pieces of land were to be set aside for schools. Slavery was not permitted north of the Ohio River. When enough settlers had moved into an area, the population could take part in the national government as a territory. When the territory reached a certain population, the region could become a state.

Before the American Revolution, American merchants traded primarily with Britain. After the war the United States was independent of Britain, and the two nations had to negotiate rules for their trade. In December 1783, while he was still in Congress, Jefferson wrote a plan for trading with Britain. A few months later, in May 1784, Congress was ready to send Jefferson abroad to help ambassadors John Adams and Benjamin Franklin negotiate trade agreements with Britain, France, and other European countries. The Treaty of Paris, which officially ended the American Revolution, had been finalized in September 1783, long before Jefferson arrived in France.

On July 5, 1784, Jefferson and his eleven-year-old daughter Martha sailed to France from Boston, Massachusetts, on the ship *Ceres*. They arrived in Paris on August 6. Jefferson's friend the Marquis de Lafayette, a French noble who had fought with the Continental army during the war, helped Jefferson to locate a suitable school for Martha. Her two sisters,

Nicolas Raguenet and Jean Baptiste depicted the Place de Greve, which is situated along the Seine River in Paris, France, in 1750. Jefferson was confident of the prospects for trade between France and the United States. He wrote the Count de Vergennes, the French foreign minister, in 1785, "No two countries are better calculated for the exchanges of commerce. France wants rice, tobacco, potash, furs, and ship-timber. We want wines, brandies, oils, and manufactures."

Maria and Lucy, were too young to travel and stayed in Virginia with relatives who lived near Richmond. Jefferson also brought one of his slaves with him to Europe so that the man might learn the art of French cooking. The slave's name was James Hemings.

In January 1785, Jefferson learned that his youngest daughter, Lucy, had died in Virginia of whooping cough the previous fall. Jefferson brought his daughter Maria to France so that his remaining family could be together. James Hemings's younger sister Sally accompanied Maria on her voyage to Paris.

Sally Hemings was born in 1773, on the plantation owned by John Wayles, who was also rumored to be her father. When John Wayles died, all his property, including his slaves, went to his daughter Martha, Jefferson's wife.

Around 1776, the entire Hemings family had come to live at Monticello. If indeed Sally and James Hemings were John Wayles's unacknowledged children, they also would have been Martha and Maria Jefferson's uncle and aunt.

In Europe, Jefferson made treaties for trade with France, Morocco, and Prussia, which later became a part of present-day Germany. During his stay in Paris, Jefferson published his only book, called *Notes on the State of Virginia*, which he had begun writing in 1781. Jefferson first printed a few hundred copies in

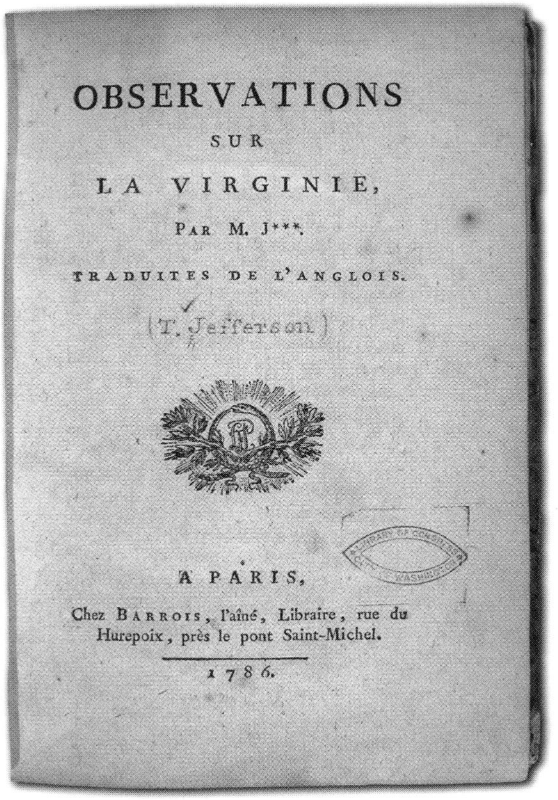

OBSERVATIONS
SUR
LA VIRGINIE,
PAR M. J***.
TRADUITES DE L'ANGLOIS.
(T. Jefferson)
A PARIS,
Chez BARROIS, l'aîné, Libraire, rue du Hurepoix, près le pont Saint-Michel.
1786.

Thomas Jefferson first printed *Notes on the State of Virginia* in Paris in 1785. The French translation of this book, called *Observations Sur La Virginie*, displeased Jefferson. He felt that his text had been translated poorly into French. The title page was printed with the wrong publication date.

France in 1785 for his friends. In 1787, Jefferson authorized two publications of his book. One printing was in London, England, and the other printing was in Paris, where *Notes* was translated into French. Jefferson's book discussed the land, the rivers, the history, and the people of his home state. *Notes* also included chapters supporting religious liberty and denouncing the practice of slavery in Virginia.

Back in Virginia, the state committee that was charged with creating a design for the new capitol

The Maison Carrée at Nîmes, France, painted by Hubert Robert between 1786 and 1787, was erected by the Roman emperor Augustus Caesar near the end of the first century B.C.

building in Richmond asked for Jefferson's help in March 1785. Jefferson admired a beautiful Roman temple in Nîmes, France. He wrote the design committee that the little temple, called the Maison Carrée, had been built "in the time of the Caesars" and was "the most perfect and precious remain of antiquity in existence."

The Maison Carrée inspired Jefferson's design and he finished his plans for the capitol building in January 1786. Along with his architectural drawing, he shipped a plaster model of the building to show the planners what the building should look like. The capitol building of Virginia was completed in 1788.

The capitol building in Richmond, Virginia, was photographed in 1865. Thomas Jefferson was assisted in his designs for this building by the French architect Charles-Louis Clérisseau.

In 1789, the citizens of France began a revolt against their king, Louis XVI. Many French citizens were inspired by the American Revolution and wanted to change their monarchy into a democratic form of government. They respected the promises of "life, liberty, and the pursuit of happiness" in Jefferson's Declaration of Independence. French revolutionaries admired the idea that "all men are created equal." Jefferson helped the rebels to write the Declaration of the Rights of Man and of the Citizen. This document championed the ideals of "liberty, equality, and fraternity" for all French citizens.

Although Thomas Jefferson supported the French Revolution, he doubted that the people of France were ready for a government similar to America's. Jefferson suggested a constitutional monarchy like that of Britain. France, he thought, needed both a king to rule the nation and an elected legislature to make just laws

Queen Marie Antoinette, the wife of the French king Louis XVI, was sketched by Jacques Louis David on October 16, 1793, on her way to be executed. The king had been killed in January of that year.

that would protect the French people.

Once the French Revolution began in 1789, it quickly became far more violent than the American Revolution had been. Royalists who supported the king fought against the citizens who opposed the monarchy. When the king's army lost the fight, Louis XVI and his queen, Marie Antoinette, were put to death during what became known as the Reign of Terror. Thousands of French men and women were killed in the struggle that followed.

On the other side of the Atlantic Ocean, the United States continued to reform its government. During the winter of 1785 and 1786, Jefferson's political ally James Madison finally convinced the state

The first ten amendments to the U.S. Constitution are known as the Bill of Rights.

These amendments were adopted in 1791, to guarantee the rights of individuals and to uphold the powers of the states against potential abuse by the federal government.

Among the first ten amendments are: freedom of speech and religion; the right for citizens to gather in public assembly; freedom of the press; the right to bear arms, or weapons; a citizen's right to a trial by jury; and protection from unreasonable searches and seizure of property.

of Virginia to adopt the Statute for Religious Freedom, which Jefferson had written a few years earlier. In the summer of 1787, an important convention was organized in Philadelphia to draft a constitution for the United States. James Madison was responsible for writing much of this new plan for the federal government. When Madison sent Jefferson a copy of the Constitution, Jefferson responded in a December 1787 letter that it was basically sound but that the Constitution still required a bill of rights. Jefferson believed that a bill of rights that defined the rights of the people and the states would help to prevent the federal government from becoming a tyranny.

8. Secretary of State

After living in Paris for five years, Thomas Jefferson and his family left France for home in October 1789. Their trip across the Atlantic Ocean to North America took twenty-six days. The Jeffersons returned to Monticello on December 23, 1789. By then the United States was operating under its new Constitution and George Washington had been elected as the nation's first president. Washington asked Jefferson to become his secretary of state. As secretary of state, Jefferson was responsible for America's relations with foreign nations. Alexander Hamilton, a delegate from New York to the Constitutional Convention, was selected as the administration's secretary of the treasury, a post that required Hamilton to oversee the government's financial policies.

Alexander Hamilton and Thomas Jefferson had different ideas about what was best for the future of America. Jefferson wanted America to become a land of independent farmers. Hamilton wanted to encourage the growth of factories, cities, and trade. These two men also interpreted the U.S. Constitution differently.

This 1879 engraving of President Washington's 1789 cabinet, or presidential advisers, was based on an earlier work by Alonzo Chappel. From left to right are Henry Knox, Thomas Jefferson, Edmund Jennings Randolph, Alexander Hamilton, and George Washington.

Thomas Jefferson felt that the Constitution gave only limited and specific powers to the central government. He wanted to protect the freedom of U.S. citizens by keeping the federal government small and allowing the states to control their own affairs.

Alexander Hamilton wanted a strong national government. He believed that the Constitution allowed the government to promote trade, banking, and manufacturing. Hamilton believed that the government should borrow money to achieve these goals, as they would ultimately aid the entire nation. Jefferson thought that borrowing large amounts of money was dangerous to the liberty of future generations. "The earth belongs always to the living generation," he said. Governments should not build up debts that the children of future generations would be required to pay off.

Hamilton admired the constitutional monarchy of Britain and wanted the United States to work closely with the British. Jefferson favored France and its republican government, which did not have a king. Furthermore, Jefferson wanted the United States to stay out of European affairs and to remain neutral in foreign disputes. Jefferson's and Hamilton's opinions on foreign and domestic policy were very different. They both tried to persuade President Washington to support their ideas.

When the Constitution was first written, Americans hoped that everyone in the nation would work together for the good of all. Many of the men who wrote the Constitution thought that political factions, or groups within the government that held to a particular opinion, might promote dissent among the population. Politicians were to care for the public good, rather than to promote their own interests. National unity would suffer if people organized themselves into little groups in opposition to one another. However, when American voters had to choose between Jefferson's and Hamilton's conflicting plans, political parties quickly developed in the new nation as citizens disagreed about important issues.

Hamilton's supporters were known as Federalists because they supported a strong federal government as well as the promotion of manufacturing, trade, and the expansion of cities. Jefferson's supporters were known as Republicans. The Republicans supported agriculture, state governments, and personal liberty. The Federalists were strong in the states of Massachusetts, Connecticut,

James Akin created this 1804 cartoon of Thomas Jefferson and Sally Hemings. Jefferson's rumored relationship with Sally Hemings, a slave at Monticello, was ridiculed by Jefferson's political foes in the press.

This 1793 Federalist cartoon *A Peep into the Antifederal Club* depicts Thomas Jefferson *(the tallest figure)* proclaiming, in a speech that patterns itself on a monologue from Shakespeare's *Hamlet,* "Whether tis nobler in the mind to knock down dry goods with this hammer: or with this head contrive some means of knocking down a government."

and New York, while the Republicans were strong in Virginia and the other southern states and Pennsylvania.

Each party sponsored newspapers that attacked the other party. The editor of the *Gazette of the United States* endorsed Hamilton. The editor of the *National Gazette* supported Jefferson. Both parties rewarded their newspapers by giving the loyal editors government jobs. The Treasury Department hired the editor who endorsed Hamilton for all its projects that required printing. The editor who endorsed Jefferson held a minor job as a translator for the State Department. This practice of offering an individual employment in exchange for a political favor or an alliance is known as patronage.

International politics became complicated during Washington's administration. France, while still in the throes of revolution, declared war on several European nations, including Britain. When France and Britain went to war in 1793, Americans tried to stay neutral. Public debate between the Federalists and Republicans became heated and nasty after news about the bloody events of the French Revolution reached American shores. "Behold France," warned a Federalist from Massachusetts, "with sufferings and crimes, in which we see . . . perhaps our future state." Jefferson said he was ready to see "half the earth desolated" rather than allow the French revolutionaries to fail. The French, Jefferson believed, were fighting for "the liberty of the whole earth."

President Washington knew that both Hamilton and Jefferson were talented men. Their disagreements over government policies, however, were so deep that they could not trust each other, let alone work together. By the autumn of 1792, Jefferson was ready to resign. Hamilton's programs, he told Washington, "flowed from principles adverse to liberty." They were intended, Jefferson thought, "to undermine and demolish the Republic." Washington needed Jefferson's help with world affairs and he asked Jefferson to continue on as his secretary of state for just one more year.

9. Vice President and President

At the end of 1793, Thomas Jefferson stepped down from his post as secretary of state and retired to Monticello. He was fifty years old and considered his retirement from public life to be permanent. Jefferson cancelled his subscription to most of the country's newspapers and devoted himself to farming.

Every day Jefferson rode through the forests and fields of Albemarle County. He began again to expand and remodel Monticello. Jefferson built a mill, along the Rivanna River, in which his slaves ground grain into flour. Hoping to bring much-needed additional income to Monticello, Jefferson set up a factory to make nails and then sold them to local farmers.

Jefferson was happy to have returned to his home in Virginia. He was close to his library and far away from the "din of politics."

Next spread: Jefferson Vail created this 1821 watercolor of Monticello. In an April 1794 letter to John Adams, Jefferson wrote, "I return to farming with an ardor which I scarcely knew in my youth, and which has got the better entirely of my love of study. . . ."

As Washington prepared to leave office in 1797, Jefferson hoped that his friend James Madison would run for the presidency. The Constitution of the United States had created a two-step procedure for electing the president and the vice president. First the citizens or the members of the legislature chose a small group of men from their state to serve in the electoral college. The number of electors each state was allowed was equal to the state's total number of congressmen and senators. In most states the legislature chose the electors. In a few states the citizens cast ballots for electors.

After being chosen, the electors from each state met at their state capitol to cast a vote for the two best candidates for the election. The head of the Senate in Washington, D.C., counted their votes in front of the members of the Senate and the House of Representatives. The man with the most votes became president. The man with the second-highest number of votes became vice president.

This system of voting did not encourage a candidate's election based on political parties. When the electoral college cast its ballots in the election of 1796, Federalist John Adams of Massachusetts got 71 votes and was declared president. The Republicans convinced Thomas Jefferson to be their candidate for president, but he received only 68 votes and was therefore named vice president. President Adams appointed members of his own Federalist Party as cabinet officers, or advisers to the president. He appointed men who had held the same posts in President Washington's administration.

As the leader of the Republican Party, Vice President Jefferson did not have an active role in Adams's Federalist administration, except for one important function. According to the Constitution, the vice president serves as the presiding officer of the Senate. As presiding officer, the vice president was only allowed to cast a vote in the Senate in the event of a tie. When Jefferson became vice president he discovered that although the Senate had "formed some rules for its own government," many decisions were left to the presiding officer.

Jefferson wanted to encourage fair debate over laws and treaties in the Senate. "Some known system of rules" would make the day-to-day work of the Senate more efficient and polite. For this purpose Jefferson compiled *A Manual of Parliamentary Practice* between 1797 and 1800. More than two hundred years later the government of the United States still follows Jefferson's *Manual* for its basic rules of procedure.

Jefferson and Adams had different political opinions. Jefferson's support of France fueled his opponents' criticism of him during the Adams administration. Many Federalists used the French revolutionaries' attacks on traditional Christianity to find fault with Jefferson. They compared Jefferson's religious beliefs to those of Maximilien Robespierre, the French leader during the bloody Reign of Terror in France.

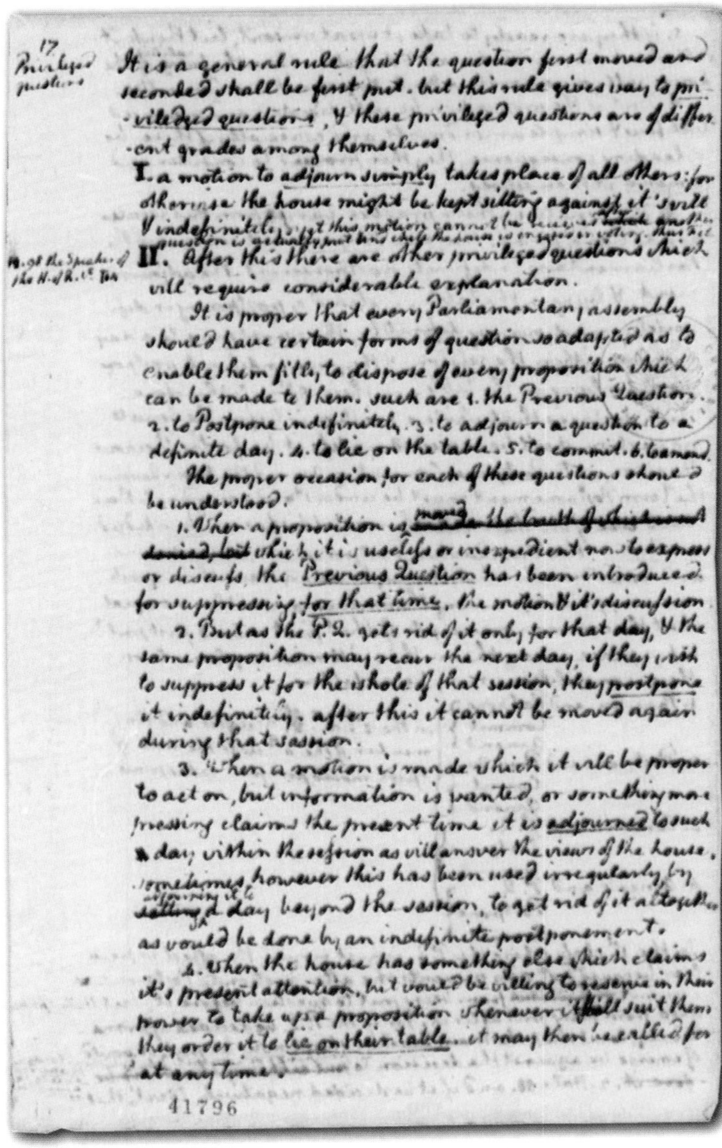

17 Privileged questions

It is a general rule that the question first moved and seconded shall be first put. but this rule gives way to privileged questions, & these privileged questions are of different grades among themselves.

I. a motion to adjourn simply takes place of all others; for otherwise the house might be kept sitting against it's will & indefinitely. yet this motion cannot be received [illegible]

[illegible] II. After this there are other privileged questions which will require considerable explanation.

It is proper that every Parliamentary assembly should have certain forms of question so adapted as to enable them fitly to dispose of every proposition which can be made to them. such are 1. the Previous Question. 2. to Postpone indefinitely. 3. to adjourn a question to a definite day. 4. to lie on the table. 5. to commit. 6. to amend.

The proper occasion for each of these questions should be understood.

1. When a proposition is [illegible] which it is useless or inexpedient now to express or discuss, the Previous Question has been introduced for suppressing for that time, the motion & it's discussion.

2. But as the P.Q. gets rid of it only for that day, & the same proposition may recur the next day, if they wish to suppress it for the whole of that session, they postpone it indefinitely. after this it cannot be moved again during that session.

3. When a motion is made which it will be proper to act on, but information is wanted, or something more pressing claims the present time it is adjourned to such day within the session as will answer the views of the house. sometimes however this has been used irregularly by adjourning it to a day beyond the session, to get rid of it altogether as would be done by an indefinite postponement.

4. When the house has something else which claims it's present attention, but would be willing to reserve in their power to take up a proposition whenever it shall suit them, they order it to lie on their table. it may then be called for at any time.

41796

Thomas Jefferson wrote this draft of *A Manual of Parliamentary Practice* around 1799. His *Manual* outlined the rules, practices, and etiquette that members of the legislature should follow. For example, legislators have a right to read any literature that pertains to a bill before voting on it. When a question of importance is raised, positive comments on an issue are heard first and negative comments are heard second.

Federalist politicians claimed that Jefferson's religious and political ideas would bring similar violence to the United States.

Republican orators and editors criticized Federalist officials in the Adams administration as well. The disputes between the two parties became so heated that in 1798, the Federalists in Congress passed the Alien and Sedition Acts. These laws were aimed at the Republican Party and its supporters.

The Sedition Act of 1798 made it illegal for anyone to criticize the president or the administration of the United States. Criticism of the vice president was still allowed, however. The Federalists who wrote the Sedition Act did not want to protect Jefferson or the members of his party.

One Republican congressman from Vermont, Matthew Lyon, who had criticized President Adams in print, was imprisoned but still managed to win his 1799 reelection campaign from his jail cell. Foreign-born journalists, many of whom supported the Republicans, were singled out for attack under this new law.

The Alien Act of 1798 gave President Adams the authority to send home or to jail any noncitizen he thought dangerous. The government prosecuted many people who were critical of it and sentenced them to jail.

Thomas Jefferson and his fellow Virginian ally James Madison believed that the Alien and Sedition Acts were unconstitutional. The problem was that if

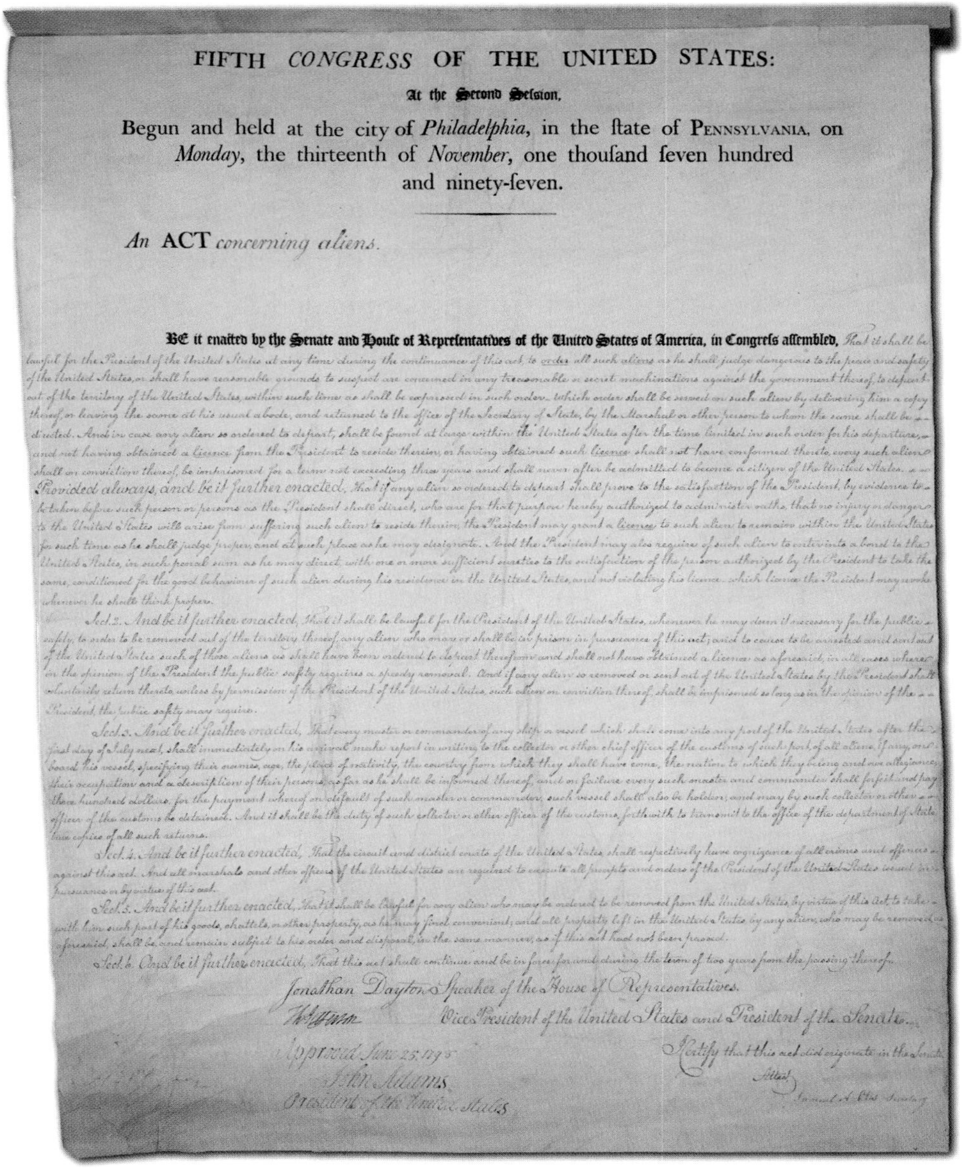

FIFTH *CONGRESS* OF THE UNITED STATES:

At the Second Seſsion,

Begun and held at the city of *Philadelphia*, in the ſtate of PENNSYLVANIA, on *Monday*, the thirteenth of *November*, one thouſand ſeven hundred and ninety-ſeven.

An ACT *concerning aliens.*

BE it enacted by the Senate and Houſe of Repreſentatives of the United States of America, in Congreſs aſſembled, That it shall be lawful for the President of the United States at any time during the continuance of this act, to order all such aliens as he shall judge dangerous to the peace and safety of the United States, or shall have reasonable grounds to suspect are concerned in any treasonable or secret machinations against the government thereof, to depart out of the territory of the United States, within such time as shall be expressed in such order. which order shall be served on such alien by delivering him a copy thereof, or leaving the same at his usual abode, and returned to the office of the Secretary of State, by the Marshal or other person to whom the same shall be directed. And in case any alien so ordered to depart, shall be found at large within the United States after the time limited in such order for his departure, and not having obtained a licence from the President to reside therein, or having obtained such licence shall not have conformed thereto, every such alien shall on conviction thereof, be imprisoned for a term not exceeding three years and shall never after be admitted to become a citizen of the United States. Provided always, and be it further enacted, That if any alien so ordered to depart shall prove to the satisfaction of the President, by evidence to be taken before such person or persons as the President shall direct, who are for that purpose hereby authorized to administer oaths, that no injury or danger to the United States will arise from suffering such alien to reside therein, the President may grant a licence to such alien to remain within the United States for such time as he shall judge proper, and at such place as he may designate. And the President may also require of such alien to enter into a bond to the United States, in such penal sum as he may direct, with one or more sufficient sureties to the satisfaction of the person authorized by the President to take the same, conditioned for the good behaviour of such alien during his residence in the United States, and not violating his licence. which licence the President may revoke whenever he shall think proper.

Sect. 2. And be it further enacted, That it shall be lawful for the President of the United States, whenever he may deem it necessary for the public safety, to order to be removed out of the territory thereof, any alien who may or shall be in prison in pursuance of this act; and to cause to be arrested and sent out of the United States such of those aliens as shall have been ordered to depart therefrom and shall not have obtained a licence as aforesaid, in all cases where in the opinion of the President the public safety requires a speedy removal. And if any alien so removed or sent out of the United States by the President shall voluntarily return thereto, unless by permission of the President of the United States, such alien on conviction thereof, shall be imprisoned so long as in the opinion of the President, the public safety may require.

Sect. 3. And be it further enacted, That every master or commander of any ship or vessel which shall come into any port of the United States after the first day of July next, shall immediately on his arrival make report in writing to the collector or other chief officer of the customs of such port, of all aliens, if any, on board his vessel, specifying their names, age, the place of nativity, the country from which they shall have come, the nation to which they belong and owe allegiance, their occupation and a description of their persons, as far as he shall be informed thereof, and on failure every such master and commander shall forfeit and pay three hundred dollars, for the payment whereof on default of such master or commander, such vessel shall also be holden, and may by such collector or other officer of the customs be detained. And it shall be the duty of such collector or other officer of the customs, forthwith to transmit to the office of the department of State true copies of all such returns.

Sect. 4. And be it further enacted, That the circuit and district courts of the United States, shall respectively have cognizance of all crimes and offences against this act. And all marshals and other officers of the United States are required to execute all precepts and orders of the President of the United States issued in pursuance or by virtue of this act.

Sect. 5. And be it further enacted, That it shall be lawful for any alien who may be ordered to be removed from the United States, by virtue of this act, to take with him such part of his goods, chattels, or other property, as he may find convenient; and all property left in the United States by any alien, who may be removed as aforesaid, shall be, and remain subject to his order and disposal, in the same manner, as if this act had not been passed.

Sect. 6. And be it further enacted, That this act shall continue and be in force for and during the term of two years from the passing thereof.

Jonathan Dayton Speaker of the House of Representatives.

Th: Jefferson Vice President of the United States and President of the Senate.

Approved June 25. 1798

John Adams

President of the United States

I certify that this act did originate in the Senate

Attest

Samuel A. Otis Secretary

The Alien Act of July 1798 was enacted by the fifth U.S. Congress. In response to this act, Thomas Jefferson wrote the 1798 Kentucky Resolution on behalf of the Commonwealth of Kentucky. This formal statement proclaimed, "this commonwealth does now enter against [the Alien and Sedition Acts], its SOLEMN PROTEST."

they criticized the government, they too might be thrown in jail for sedition. Therefore, in secret, Thomas Jefferson wrote a long statement that explained why the Alien and Sedition Acts were illegal and posed a threat to American freedom.

Jefferson sent his statement to his Republican friends who were powerful in the Kentucky legislature. Without identifying the author, on November 16, 1798, members of the Kentucky legislature adopted the Kentucky Resolution, which declared that any state had the right to oppose actions by the federal government that went against the Constitution. James Madison wrote a similar essay for the legislature of Virginia, which passed the Virginia Resolution on December 24, 1798.

Jefferson's argument against the Alien and Sedition Acts went even further than Madison's did. The Kentucky Resolution claimed that states had the right to nullify, or cancel, any federal law the state regarded as unconstitutional.

In 1798, Thomas Jefferson learned that some Pennsylvanians wanted to start an insurrection against the Alien and Sedition Acts. Jefferson warned them against it and advised the protesters to use a more peaceful form of resistance. Violence, he told his friend Edmund Pendleton in 1799, was "not the kind of opposition the American people will permit." A better way to fight bad government, Jefferson counseled his friend, was "by the constitutional means of election and petition."

Thomas Jefferson's knowledge of the American people proved accurate. The people's negative reaction to the Alien and Sedition Acts swept Jefferson and his party into office in the election of 1800. Once again, however, the electoral college caused problems for the election. The Republican candidates for president and vice president were, respectively, Thomas Jefferson, of Virginia, and Aaron Burr, of New York. When the electoral ballots were counted, the Federalists John Adams and South Carolina's Charles C. Pinckney had

This 1801 victory banner celebrating Thomas Jefferson's election to the presidency reads "Jefferson President of the United States of America. John Adams is no more."

65 and 64 votes, respectively. One Federalist elector had cast his ballot for John Jay, of New York. Jefferson and Burr ended up in a tie, with 73 electoral votes each.

Aaron Burr was ambitious and prone to intrigue. Although Burr had run as the Republican candidate for vice president, he was suddenly given the chance to become president. When no candidate wins a clear majority in the electoral college, the Constitution states that the House of Representatives must immediately decide who will be president. Some Federalists hated Jefferson more than they disliked Burr and were ready to use their votes to keep Jefferson out of the White House by electing Burr. The votes were tallied by state, with each state getting one vote. The nation had sixteen states in 1800, and a majority of nine state votes was required for a candidate to win. Day after day the House of Representatives met and voted. Eight states wanted Jefferson, and six states wanted Burr. The congressmen from Maryland and Vermont were evenly divided on their choice and could not reach a decision.

Thirty-five times the congressmen cast their ballots without obtaining a majority for either candidate. Rumors swept through the halls of Congress and across the nation as the deadlock continued. Would the election be stolen from Jefferson? Finally, on the thirty-sixth ballot held on February 17, 1801, the deadlock was broken when James A. Bayard, the Federalist representative from Delaware, submitted a blank ballot rather than casting a vote for Burr. With the majority of states voting for Jefferson, he was elected U.S. president.

Although the U.S. Constitution had survived this crisis caused by a tie in the electoral college, to avoid the same problem in the future, a twelfth amendment to the Constitution was later adopted in 1804. From then on, electors voted separately for the president and vice president.

On Wednesday, March 4, 1801, fifty-seven-year-old Thomas Jefferson walked from his boardinghouse to the unfinished U.S. Capitol, which was being constructed

William Birch did this watercolor of the Capitol in Washington, D.C., around 1800. Jefferson had successfully lobbied to build the new U.S. capital in a rural area rather than a metropolis such as New York City so that it would better reflect the young nation's ties to agriculture.

Caleb Boyle painted Thomas Jefferson standing before the Natural Bridge around 1801. The bridge is actually a massive stone arch that looks like a bridge. Jefferson was so fascinated by Virginia's Natural Bridge that he purchased land in the southern Shenandoah Valley that included this rock formation in 1774.

near the Potomac River. He was the first president to be inaugurated in Washington, D.C. An inauguration is the ceremony at which an elected official is sworn into government office. Jefferson's distant cousin Chief Justice John Marshall administered the oath of office. In his inaugural address, Thomas Jefferson reminded his fellow citizens that "every difference of opinion is not a difference of principle." Jefferson proclaimed that "we are all Republicans—we are all Federalists." Rather than throwing critics of the government into jail for sedition, Jefferson declared that they should be free to speak their mind. "If there be any among us who would wish to dissolve this Union or to change its republican form, let them stand undisturbed as . . . [proof that] error of opinion may be tolerated where reason is left free to combat it."

10. Louisiana for a Song

The city of New Orleans is located near the mouth of the Mississippi River. The busy port of New Orleans controlled the movement of ships and cargoes from the Mississippi into the Gulf of Mexico. Each autumn farmers in Kentucky, Tennessee, and Ohio loaded their produce and meat onto flatboats and floated them down the Ohio River to the Mississippi River and then down to New Orleans.

The United States had signed a treaty with Spain, in 1795, that allowed Americans to land their flour, pork, and other farm products at New Orleans, as the port city was then a Spanish possession. Each year the city's merchants paid about $3 million for American products and then exported them on oceangoing ships bound for world markets.

On October 16, 1802, a Spanish official at New Orleans closed the Mississippi River to American vessels. As news of this action spread up the river, Americans in the area reacted with anger. Spain was violating the treaty. How would farmers get their goods

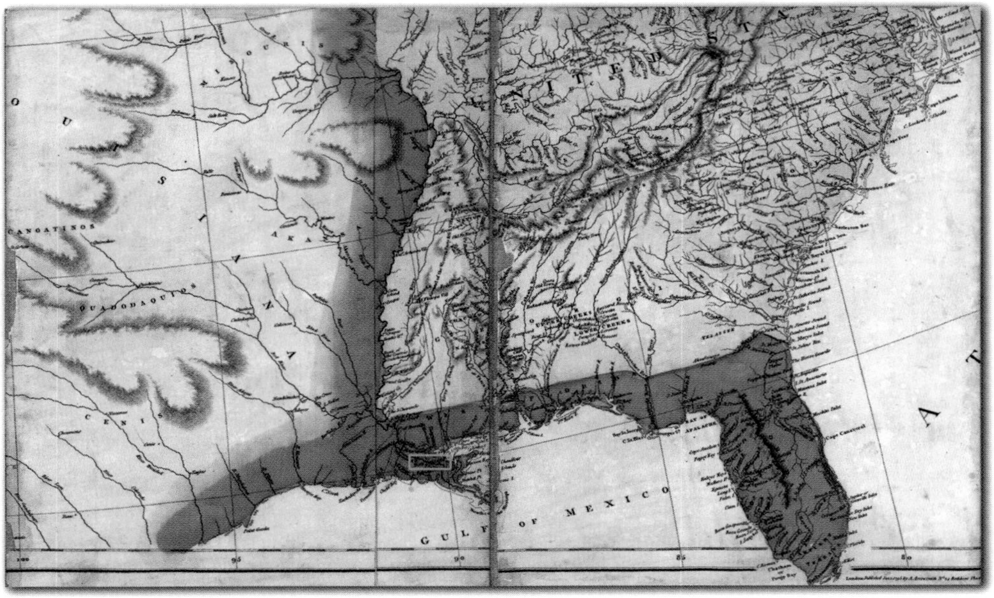

This 1795 map of North America was published in London by A. Arrowsmith. According to Arrowsmith the map featured "all the new discoveries in the interior parts of North America." The area in blue traces the flow of the Mississippi River. The pink square is the approximate location of New Orleans.

to market, and what would happen to the farmer's produce if they could not sell it to buyers in New Orleans?

By 1802, the French Revolution had finally ended and General Napoléon Bonaparte had taken control of France. Napoléon hoped to extend his empire in North America. He wanted France to import sugar from the island of Hispaniola, which is modern-day Haiti and the Dominican Republic. He also wanted to take possession of the Louisiana Territory so that the food and supplies grown in that region could be shipped to Hispaniola.

These supplies would be used to sustain the slaves and plantation owners who grew sugarcane on the plantations of Hispaniola. Furthermore, a French claim to land in North America would offset the growing power of the United States. The Louisiana Territory was vast and included all the land from the Mississippi River west to the Rocky Mountains and from New Orleans up to Canada.

Americans were aware that in 1800 Napoléon had negotiated with Spain to obtain the Louisiana Territory. Americans also knew that Napoléon had sent troops across the Atlantic Ocean to take control of Spanish Hispaniola and that he was planning to take possession of Louisiana, too. Americans speculated that perhaps Napoléon had told Spain to close the Mississippi River. Spanish control of New Orleans had been weak. Napoléon's armies, however, were among the strongest in the world. If Napoléon were to keep the Mississippi River's port in New Orleans closed, American farmers along the Ohio River would be ruined because they could not send their goods to market in New Orleans.

Over a period of days and weeks, the news that Spain had closed the port of New Orleans spread throughout the nation. By November 1802, President Jefferson and Congress learned what had happened in New Orleans. Some Americans wanted to declare war on France and thought that President Jefferson should

Antoine Jean Gros painted General Napoléon Bonaparte on the Bridge of Arcole in Italy around 1796. On November 17, 1796, the French, under the leadership of General Napoléon Bonaparte, pushed back the Austrian army from the town of Arcole. Napoléon hoped to expand the French Empire by conquering other empires and the territories in their possession.

send an army to capture New Orleans before Napoléon's troops arrived there.

Jefferson wanted to avoid war with France. His diplomat in Paris, Robert R. Livingston, had been negotiating with Napoléon for more than one year. Livingston had tried to convince the general that France did not need Louisiana, as American farmers could sell France all the supplies the French needed for the sugar plantations on Hispaniola.

On Monday, January 10, 1803, negotiations with France took another turn. President Jefferson sent an urgent note to James Monroe, who had just finished his second term as governor of Virginia. "I have but a moment to inform you," the president wrote, "that the fever into which the western mind is thrown by the affair at N[ew] Orleans . . . threatens to overbear our peace." Jefferson asked Monroe to drop everything and sail for France.

Monroe and Livingston were instructed to buy New Orleans and the land along the Gulf of Mexico, then known as West Florida, from the French. This region includes the coastal areas of the present-day states of Mississippi and Alabama, and the western end of the Florida panhandle. Congress had set aside $2 million as an advance payment, but Jefferson instructed Monroe that he could negotiate the purchase up to an amount of almost $10 million. If Napoléon took possession of New Orleans, Jefferson wrote in his note to

Monroe, the United States would be forced to ally itself with Britain against France.

On Sunday, March 6, 1803, Monroe and his family loaded their baggage aboard a ship in New York City. One month later, on Friday, April 8, 1803, they sailed into the French harbor at Le Havre. An honor guard of fifty French soldiers accompanied the Monroes to their hotel. That same day, 100 miles (161 km) away in Paris, Napoléon Bonaparte was reading newspapers from America and Britain. These publications were filled with articles concerning the angry debates in Congress over the closing of the New Orleans port. If Monroe and Livingston were unable to buy New Orleans, Americans would ready themselves to capture it by force.

Napoléon quickly decided that he should sell all of Louisiana to the United States. He would use the money to fight the British. While James Monroe traveled to Paris, Napoléon sent his treasury minister, François Barbé-Marbois, to meet with Ambassador Livingston. "Do not even wait for the arrival of Mr. Monroe," Napoléon instructed Barbé-Marbois, "have an interview this very day with Mr. Livingston." Barbé-Marbois and Livingston met several times before Monroe arrived.

On April 13, Livingston and Monroe were finishing dinner at Livingston's house. Suddenly they saw someone in the garden outside the dining room. It was the French minister, Barbé-Marbois, who requested that Livingston come to his office later that evening. Monroe had not yet been introduced to Napoléon. Until Monroe had the opportunity to present his official papers to the French, he could not take part in these official talks. The next morning Livingston told Monroe that France was willing to sell all of Louisiana, not just the coastal areas, for about 80 million francs, or $15 million.

A few days later, after Monroe had been officially introduced to Napoléon, Monroe and Livingston worked with Barbé-Marbois to write a treaty. The United States would buy Louisiana at the asking price of 80 million francs. The United States would borrow the money from British and Dutch banks. The sizable interest that the British banks would earn on this large loan outweighed any ill will the British government harbored toward France, Britain's longtime enemy. Interest is the fee that a bank, or another financial institution, charges a borrower for the loan of money.

The three men signed the official treaty on May 2, 1803. The sale of Louisiana, Napoléon told them, "strengthens for ever the power of the United States. . . . I have just given to England a maritime rival that will sooner or later humble her pride." Robert R. Livingston agreed. "This is the noblest work of our whole lives," he said. "From this day the United States take their place among the powers of the first rank."

The first report of the Louisiana Purchase reached President Jefferson on July 3, 1803. As word of the astonishing transaction spread throughout the country, letters of congratulation poured into the White House. "You have bought Louisiana for a song," General Horatio Gates wrote from New York, it is "the greatest and most beneficial event that has taken place since the Declaration of Independence." A congressman from Tennessee called the Louisiana Purchase "a second Declaration of Independence." Even the French ambassador called it "the greatest achievement in the history of the United States since their independence."

The primary author of the declaration was troubled, however. Thomas Jefferson believed that the Constitution put strict limits on the power of the federal government. He felt that the Louisiana Purchase was wonderful, but he knew that the Constitution said nothing about buying half of a continent. Nor did the Constitution say anything about making thousands of French and Spanish people into American citizens. Jefferson realized that the Louisiana Purchase had gone beyond the Constitution, and he spent several weeks trying to draft an amendment to make the purchase entirely legal.

Then came a letter from Monroe and Livingston. Napoléon Bonaparte was impatient for his money and the diplomats worried that he might change his mind. There was no time to amend the Constitution. Jefferson told his allies in the Senate to approve the Louisiana Purchase treaty quickly. There was no time for debate. The Senate approved the treaty on October 20.

This 1803 gouache, which is a type of watercolor, depicts the changing of the flag at the fort of New Orleans. The French flag was taken down and the United States flag was raised after the official transfer of Louisiana from France to the United States.

Two months later, on December 20, 1803, Jefferson's representative met Napoléon's representative in New Orleans. In the Cabildo, or city hall, a building at Jackson Square that is now part of the Louisiana State Museum, they signed the papers that sold Louisiana to the United States. Months later, in St. Louis, Missouri, Napoléon's representative signed similar papers transferring the northern part of Louisiana to the United States.

No one knew how big Louisiana actually was in 1803. The next year Jefferson sent Meriwether Lewis and William Clark on an expedition to explore the northern part of the Louisiana Territory. The expedition party followed the Missouri River west to the Rocky Mountains. Then they crossed the Rockies and traveled along the Columbia River until they finally reached the Pacific Ocean. While Lewis and Clark were exploring the northern part of the Louisiana Purchase, Jefferson sent other explorers, such as Zebulon Pike and an expedition led by Thomas Freeman and Peter Custis, to investigate the Arkansas and Ouachita rivers in the southern part of the territory.

In 1805, Jefferson received a shipment of specimens and artifacts from Meriwether Lewis. This replica of a Native American shield was done by Butch Thunder Hawk and students at the United Tribes Technical College. The design is that of the Hunkpapa Lakota, members of the Sioux nation, whom the Lewis and Clark expedition likely encountered.

The United States, Spain, and Britain took sixteen years to agree on the final boundaries of the Louisiana Purchase territory. Thirteen American states would eventually be formed from this newly acquired territory: Arkansas, Colorado, Iowa, Kansas, Louisiana, Minnesota, Missouri, Montana, Nebraska, North Dakota, Oklahoma, South Dakota, and Wyoming.

When the United States paid off the loans and accumulated interest in 1823, the total cost of the Louisiana Territory was $23,527,872.57. The United States had purchased nearly 530 million acres (214.5 million ha) of land, or 828,125 square miles (2,144,834 sq km), for about four cents per acre.

11. An Active Retirement

Thomas Jefferson was reelected president in 1804 by a large majority. The vote in the electoral college was 162 ballots for Jefferson and 14 ballots for his Federalist opponent, Charles C. Pinckney of South Carolina. This type of overwhelming political victory is sometimes referred to as a landslide.

The last years of Jefferson's presidency were difficult, however. France and Britain were at war, and American ships and sailors suffered during the conflict.

British vessels often stopped American ships at sea and forced American sailors to join the British navy, as Britain needed additional manpower to fight the French on the seas. British warships also attacked American ships that traded with France.

Hoping to avoid war with Britain, Jefferson urged Congress to impose an embargo on American trade

Opposite: Gilbert Stuart painted Thomas Jefferson in 1805. Jefferson wrote to John Taylor in 1808, "Till [France and England] return to some sense of moral duty, therefore, we keep within ourselves. . . . Time may produce peace in Europe."

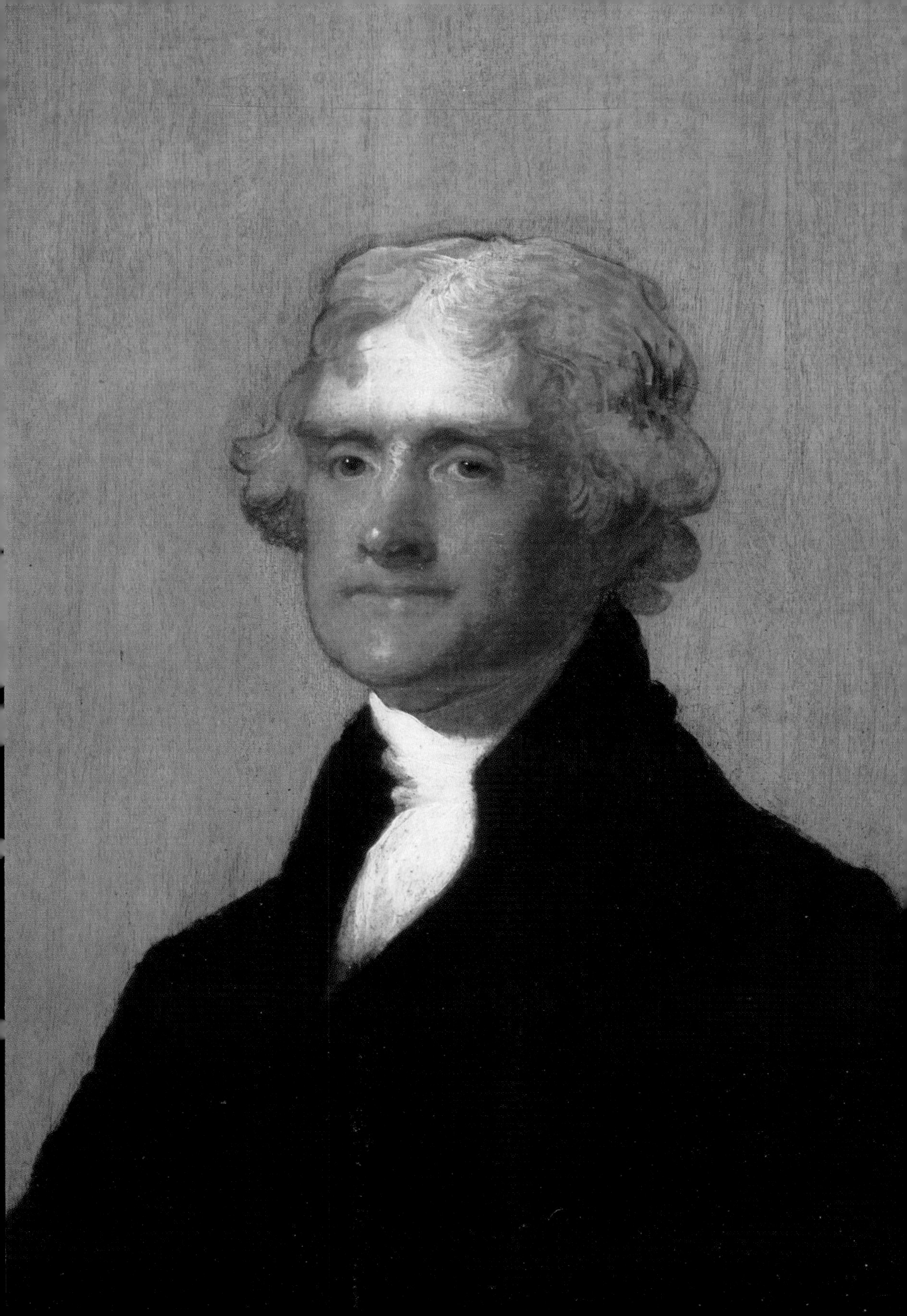

Although Jefferson managed his estate with slave labor, he did recognize that the practice of slavery was horrific. Jefferson wrote essays and lobbied for changes in the government in the hope of one day limiting slavery in America.

In his Notes on the State of Virginia *Jefferson wrote that God would punish those who engaged in slavery. Furthermore, slave-owning parents should be aware of the bad example they set for their children.*

Jefferson was the main author of the Ordinance of 1784. This congressional legislation was written to guide the formation of new states from the frontier territories in the Northwest. Jefferson's draft of the ordinance called for banning slavery in the western territories. Congress, however, voted against including this ban on slavery. Not until 1787 would slavery be banned from the western territories.

with Europe. Jefferson hoped that by refusing to ship American goods to Europe he could stop Britain and France from capturing American ships and seamen.

The embargo did not work. Farmers and manufacturers in New England were too dependent on their trade with Europe across the Atlantic Ocean. Jefferson's attempt to pressure Britain and France by stopping American trade with Europe hurt citizens of the northern states. Congress repealed the embargo a few days after Jefferson retired from the presidency on March 4, 1809. Although the new president, James Madison, also tried to remain neutral as Britain continued its war with France, the task proved impossible. In

1812, the United States declared war on Britain. British forces raided Washington, D.C., in August 1814 and burned the White House. The war later came to an end after the American general Andrew Jackson won the Battle of New Orleans on January 8, 1815.

Jefferson returned to Monticello on March 15, 1809. The last great accomplishment of Jefferson's life was the founding of the University of Virginia. Decades before, in 1779, Jefferson had drawn up plans for a system of public education. In 1819, ten years after Jefferson retired from the presidency, the legislature of Virginia finally adopted the central part of that plan. The legislature

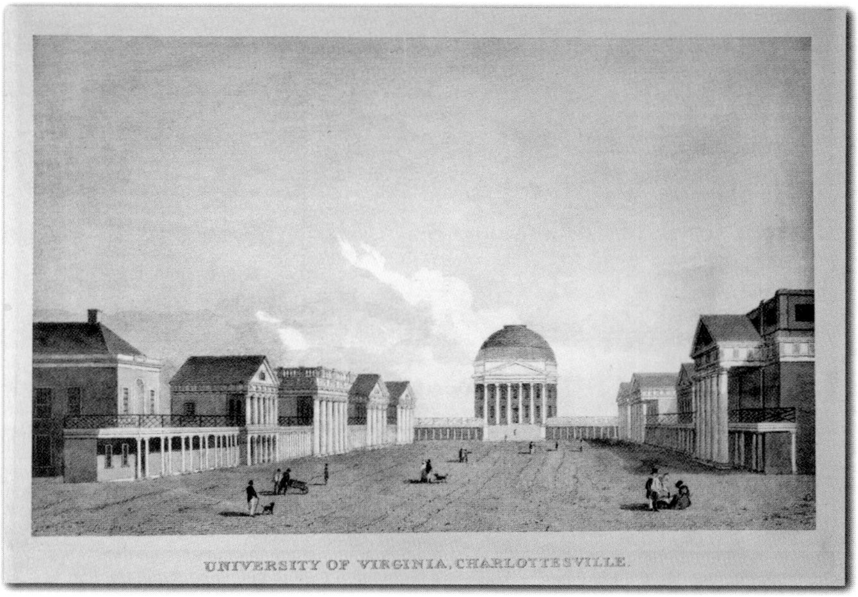

This 1825 engraving of the University of Virginia grounds was created by Peter Maverick. At the center of the engraving is the Rotunda, designed by Thomas Jefferson, which was initially used to house the college's library.

passed a law for the creation of the University of Virginia on January 25, 1819. Jefferson served as the first rector, or presiding officer, of its governing board. He also designed distinctive buildings and landscapes for the university's grounds. The University of Virginia opened its doors in Charlottesville on March 7, 1825. Jefferson told a friend that children are the leaders of the future. By "establishing an institution of wisdom for them, we secure [wisdom] to all our future generations."

July 4, 1826, was the fiftieth anniversary of the Declaration of Independence. It was also the day that both Thomas Jefferson and John Adams died. Although Jefferson's greatest success as president was the Louisiana Purchase, he chose to place three other accomplishments on his tombstone. Jefferson wanted to be remembered as the author of the Declaration of Independence, the author of the Virginia Statute for Religious Freedom, and the father of the University of Virginia.

Jefferson was a firm believer in political freedom, religious liberty, and education. These were his legacies to the American people. Perhaps they were what John Adams had in mind when he spoke his last words: "Thomas Jefferson survives." Adams was, however, probably only stating what he believed to be true. The two men had overcome their political rivalry and wrote to each other extensively in later years, often to express their hopes and concerns for America's future.

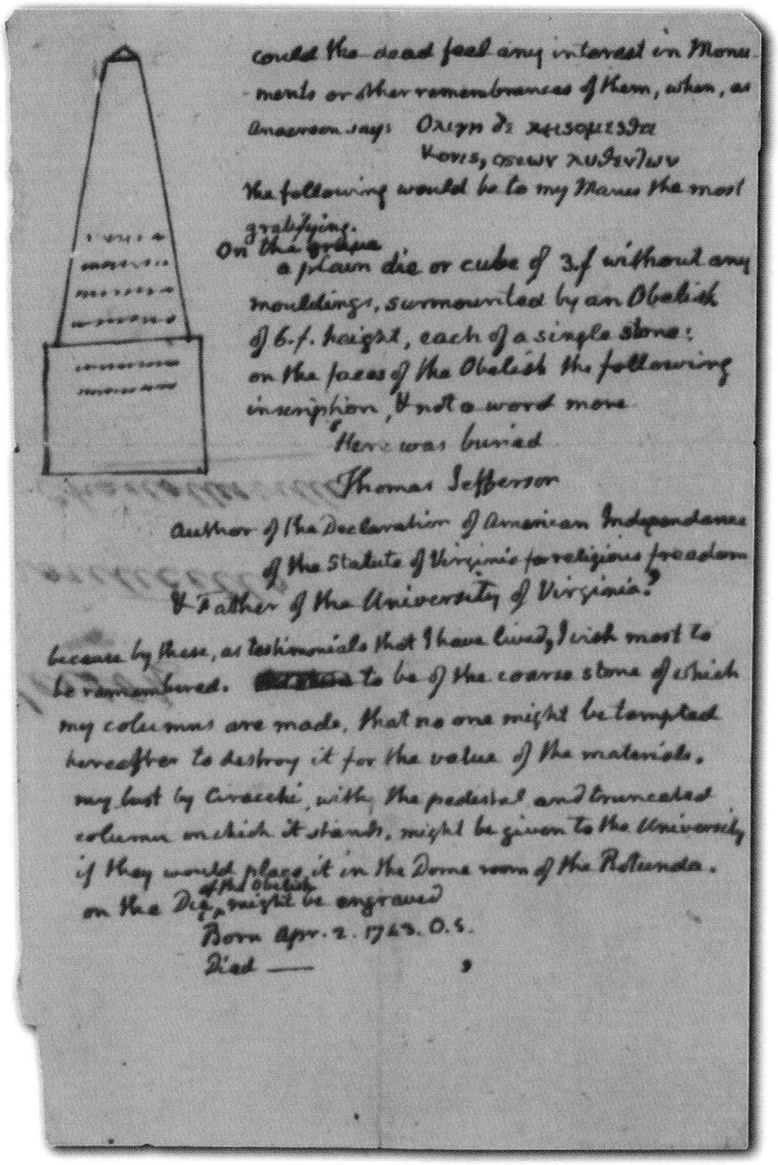

could the dead feel any interest in Monu-
-ments or other remembrances of them, when, as
Anacreon says Ὀλίγη δὲ κεισόμεσθα
κόνις, ὀστέων λυθέντων
the following would be to my Manes the most
gratifying.
On the grave
a plain die or cube of 3.f without any
mouldings, surmounted by an Obelisk
of 6.f. height, each of a single stone:
on the faces of the Obelisk the following
inscription, & not a word more
'Here was buried
Thomas Jefferson
Author of the Declaration of American Independance
of the Statute of Virginia for religious freedom
& Father of the University of Virginia.'
because by these, as testimonials that I have lived, I wish most to
be remembered. to be of the coarse stone of which
my columns are made, that no one might be tempted
hereafter to destroy it for the value of the materials.
my bust by Ciracchi, with the pedestal and truncated
column on which it stands, might be given to the University
if they would place it in the Dome room of the Rotunda.
on the Die of the Obelisk might be engraved
Born Apr. 2. 1743. O.S.
Died ——

Thomas Jefferson drafted the epitaph for his tombstone around 1820. Once he had chosen the words that would be carved onto his tombstone, he specified that "not a word more" was to be added. An epitaph is a statement that summarizes a person's life or achievements.

On April 29, 1962, nearly 136 years after Thomas Jefferson died, U.S. president John F. Kennedy and Jacqueline Kennedy, the first lady, hosted a formal banquet in Washington, D.C. In attendance were a number of famous writers, astronauts, scientists, diplomats, and

The Jefferson Memorial in Washington, D.C., was dedicated in 1943. Under the dome is a towering bronze statue of Thomas Jefferson. Excerpts from Jefferson's writings adorn the memorial, including the Declaration of Independence and the following passage from a September 1800 letter to Dr. Benjamin Rush: "I have sworn upon the altar of God eternal hostility against every form of tyranny over the mind of man."

several winners of the Nobel Prize, a medal that is awarded to men and women for their outstanding intellectual contributions to humanity.

President Kennedy said to this distinguished gathering that this was "the most extraordinary collection of talent, of human knowledge, that has ever been gathered together at the White House, with the possible exception of when Thomas Jefferson dined alone."

Timeline

1743	Thomas Jefferson is born at Shadwell on April 13 in Albemarle County, Virginia.
1752	In 1752, Britain and the American colonies change from an old calendar to a new one that is more accurate. The old calendar was established by Julius Caesar and was called the Julian calendar. Pope Gregory created the new Gregorian calendar. According to the old Julian calendar, Thomas Jefferson was born on April 2.
1754–1763	The French and Indian War is fought.
1760	Thomas Jefferson enters the College of William and Mary in Williamsburg, Virginia.
1762	Thomas Jefferson graduates from the College of William and Mary.
1767	Thomas Jefferson passes the bar exam and becomes a lawyer.
1768	Thomas Jefferson is elected a member of the House of Burgesses.
1770	Jefferson's house and library at Shadwell burn down.
1772	Thomas Jefferson marries Martha Wayles Skelton and later moves to Monticello, his home in Charlottesville, Virginia.
1773	The British parliament passes the Tea Act. American colonists respond with the Boston Tea Party.
1774	Jefferson publishes *A Summary View of the Rights of British America* for the 1774 Virginia Convention. Parliament sends British troops to New England and New York.

1775	The Battle of Lexington and Concord begins the American Revolution.
1776	Thomas Jefferson writes the Declaration of Independence.
	Virginia adopts its first state constitution.
	Jefferson begins his term in Virginia's House of Delegates.
1779	Thomas Jefferson is elected Governor of Virginia.
	Jefferson drafts Virginia's Statue for Religious Freedom.
1781	After Benedict Arnold raids Richmond, Virginia, in January, Governor Jefferson and some of the state government officials flee to Charlottesville. The legislature then moves to Staunton.
	British lieutenant colonel Banastre Tarleton orders a raid, under the command of Captain McLeod, on Charlottesville and Monticello in June.
	Cornwallis surrenders at Yorktown, Virginia, in October, which ends the American Revolution.
1782	Martha Wayles Skelton, Jefferson's wife of ten years, dies on September 6, from complications of childbirth.
1783	Thomas Jefferson is elected to the Continental Congress.
1784	Thomas Jefferson is appointed to assist Benjamin Franklin and John Adams with negotiations in Europe.
1785	Jefferson's *Notes on the State of Virginia* is first published in France.
1786	The Statute for Religious Freedom is passed in Virginia.
1787	The Philadelphia Convention sends the U.S. Constitution to the states for ratification in September.

1790	Thomas Jefferson, appointed by President George Washington, assumes his duties as the first secretary of state under the U.S. Constitution.
1797–1801	Jefferson serves as vice president of the United States under President John Adams.
1798	Jefferson secretly writes the Kentucky Resolution against the Alien and Sedition Acts.
1801	Jefferson is elected president of the United States.
1803	The treaty between France and the United States is signed resulting in the Louisiana Purchase.
1804	Jefferson is reelected.
1807	Congress, at Jefferson's urging, imposes an embargo in an effort to avoid war with France or Britain.
1809	After James Madison takes office as president, Jefferson retires to Monticello.
1819	The University of Virginia is chartered.
1825	The University of Virginia opens.
1826	Jefferson dies at Monticello on July 4, the fiftieth anniversary of the Declaration of Independence.

Glossary

antiquity (an-TIH-kwih-tee) Ancient times, or the things and matters of ancient times.

ardor (AR-der) A feeling of passion and excitement.

aristocratic (uh-ris-tuh-KRA-tik) Relating to a member of the upper class or nobility.

avert (uh-VERT) To avoid something.

baptized (BAP-tyzd) Sprinkled someone with or immersed someone in water to show that person's acceptance into the Christian faith.

burgesses (BUR-jis-ez) Citizens elected to help rule colonial Virginia.

colleagues (KAH-leegz) People who do the same work.

defected (dih-FEKT-ed) To have given up one's loyalty to one group or country to join another.

desolated (DEH-suh-layt-ed) To have destroyed.

disme (DYM) An early form of the U.S. dime.

engrossed (in-GROHSD) To have prepared a copy of a document with fine handwriting.

ethics (EH-thiks) The study of what is good and bad and how people should behave.

etiquette (EH-tih-kit) The manners to be observed in social life.

Homer (HOH-mur) The great poet of ancient Greece who wrote two long poems, or epics, called *The Iliad* and *The Odyssey*.

hypocrisy (hih-PAH-kruh-see) Pretending to have high principles, beliefs, or feelings.

ideologies (eye-dee-AH-luh-jeez) Belief systems that can be used to explain political and social events.

import (IM-port) To bring goods into one country from another.

inflation (in-FLAY-shun) A sharp increase in the price of goods, sometimes caused by a shortage of goods.

insurrection (in-suh-REK-shun) Rebelling against someone's control, usually with weapons.

intrigue (IN-treeg) Secret plotting or scheming against an individual or a group.

legislature (LEH-jis-lay-chur) A body of people that has the power to make or pass laws.

meditation (meh-dih-TAY-shun) The act of keeping one's thoughts focused on something.

militia (muh-LIH-shuh) A group of volunteer or citizen soldiers who are organized to assemble in emergencies.

nullify (NUH-luh-fy) To make valueless.

orator (OR-uh-tur) A skilled public speaker.

parish (PAR-ish) A church community.

primitive (PRIH-muh-tiv) Something that is in an early stage of growth.

prominent (PRAH-mih-nent) Referring to something that is easy to see because it stands out in some way.

proprietors (pruh-PRY-uh-turz) People who hold or own the right to something.

rhetoric (REH-tuh-rik) The art of writing or speaking effectively.

Stamp Act (STAMP AKT) The law British parliament passed that placed a tax on paper goods in the colonies.

tyranny (TEER-uh-nee) Cruel use of power over others; a government that oppresses the people over whom it governs.

usurpations (yoo-sur-PAY-shunz) Acts of wrongfully seizing, or taking, power by force and without right.

Additional Resources

To learn more about Thomas Jefferson, check out these books and Web sites:

Books

Armstrong, Jennifer. *Thomas Jefferson: Letters from a Philadelphia Bookworm*. Delray Beach, FL: Winslow Press, 2000.

Bober, Natalie. *Thomas Jefferson: Man on a Mountain*. New York: Aladdin Paperbacks, 1997.

Web Sites

Due to the changing nature of Internet links, PowerPlus Books has developed an online list of Web sites related to the subject of this book. This site is updated regularly. Please use this link to access the list: www.powerkidslinks.com/lalt/tjefferson/

Bibliography

Adams, William Howard, ed. *The Eye of Thomas Jefferson*. Washington, D.C.: National Gallery of Art, 1976.

Boyd, Julian P., Charles Cullen, John Catanzariti, and Barbara Oberg et al., eds. *Papers of Thomas Jefferson*. 31 vols. Princeton, NJ: Princeton University Press, 1950– 2003.

Ellis, Joseph J. et al. *Thomas Jefferson: Genius of Liberty*. New York: Viking Studio in association with the Library of Congress, D.C., 2000.

Foley, John P. *The Jefferson Cyclopedia*. New York and London: Funk & Wagnells Company, 1900.

Ford, Paul Leicester, ed. *The Writings of Thomas Jefferson*. New York: Putnam's Sons, 1892–1899.

Kimball, Fiske. *The Capitol of Virginia: A Landmark of American Architecture*. Richmond, VA: Virginia State Library and Archives, 1989.

Kukla, Jon. *A Wilderness So Immense: The Louisiana Purchase and the Destiny of America*. New York: A. A. Knopf, 2003.

Maier, Pauline. *American Scripture: Making the Declaration of Independence*. New York: Knopf, 1997.

Malone, Dumas. *Jefferson and His Times*. 5 vols. Boston: Little, Brown and Company, 1948–1981.

Peterson, Merrill D., ed. *Writings/Thomas Jefferson*. New York: Viking Press, 1984.

Index

About the Authors

Amy Kukla graduated from Roanoke College in 2000. Her first book was *Patrick Henry: Voice of the Revolution*, published by the Rosen Publishing Group, Inc., in 2002. Her interest in Thomas Jefferson began as a child with annual family trips to Monticello, where she was fascinated with Jefferson's quirky inventions.

Dr. Jon Kukla graduated from Carthage College in 1970 and received his Ph.D. in history from the University of Toronto in 1980. He became director of the Patrick Henry Memorial Foundation in January 2000, after holding similar positions in New Orleans, Louisiana, and Richmond, Virginia. Dr. Kukla is an expert on early American history and is the author of *A Wilderness So Immense: The Louisiana Purchase and the Destiny of America* and coauthor with his daughter Amy of *Patrick Henry: Voice of the Revolution*.

About the Consultant

Professor Robert F. Turner holds both professional and academic doctorates from Thomas Jefferson's University of Virginia, where he has taught in both the department of government and the school of law. His interest in Thomas Jefferson dates from three decades ago, and, during 2000 and 2001, he chaired a Scholars Commission of more than a dozen distinguished scholars from around the country examining the relationship between Jefferson and one of his slaves.

Primary Sources

Cover. *Thomas Jefferson*, painting, 1791, Charles Willson Peale, Courtesy of Independence National Historical Park. Background. Engrossed copy of the Declaration of Independence, August 2, 1776, Miscellaneous Papers of the Continental Congress, 1774–1789; Records of the Continental and Confederation Congresses and the Constitutional Convention, 1774–1789, Record Group 360, National Archives and Records Administration. **Page 4**. *Thomas Jefferson*, painting, 1788, John Trumbull, The White House Collection, courtesy the White House Historical Association. **Page 6**. *View from Monticello Looking Toward Charlottesville*, watercolor, 1827, Jane Pitford Braddick Peticolas, Courtesy of Monticello/Thomas Jefferson Foundation, Inc. **Page 8**. *A map of the most inhabited part of Virginia containing the whole province of Maryland with part of Pensilvania, New Jersey and North Carolina*, drawn by Joshua Fry and Peter Jefferson in 1751, published in London by Thomas Jefferys in 1755, Library of Congress Geography and Map Division (Note: Map was adapted by addition of color and key). **Page 9**. School on Tuckahoo plantation, The Colonial Williamsburg Foundation. **Page 11**. *George Wythe Esq.*, pen and ink, April 25, 1781, John Trumbull, Print and Picture Collection, the Free Library of Philadelphia. **Page 13**. *Patrick Henry Before the House of Burgesses*, painting, 1851, Peter Rothermel, Red Hill, The Patrick Henry National Memorial. **Page 15**. *The Prayer of Voltaire*, engraving, 1700s, French school, Bibliotheque Nationale, Paris, France/Bridgeman Art Library. **Page 17**. The Life and Morals of Jesus of Nazareth, title page from Jefferson Bible, Library of Congress Rare Book and Special Collections Division. **Page 18**. List of books from Thomas Jefferson to Library of Congress, drafted Feb 27–Mar 28, 1815, Library of Congress Rare Book and Special Collections Division **Page 20**. Layette pincushion, Martha Wayles Jefferson, Courtesy of Monticello/Thomas Jefferson Foundation, Inc. **Page 21**. Elevation of the first Monticello, ink on paper, 1769–70, Thomas Jefferson, Courtesy of Monticello/Thomas Jefferson Foundation, Inc. **Page 29**. "A Summary View of the Rights of British America," Thomas Jefferson to Virginia Delegates to the Continental Congress, August 1774, Library of Congress Manuscript Division. **Page 32**. Rough Draft of the Declaration of Independence, manuscript, 1776, Thomas Jefferson, Library of Congress Manuscript Division. **Page 33**. *The House of Jacob Graff*, photograph, April 1855, Frederick DeBourg Richards Photograph Collection at the Library Company of Philadelphia Page 34. *La Destruction de la Statue Royale a Nouvelle Yorck*, hand-colored etching, circa 1770s, attributed to Andre Basset l'aine, Library of Congress Prints and Photographs Division. **Page 35**. Declaration of Independence, printed by William J. Stone, copperplate engraving, 1823, copperplate engraving, "Engraved by W.I. STONE for the Dept. of State by order/ of J.Q. ADAMS Secy of State July 4th 1823," NARA. **Page 39**. The Great Seal of Virginia, close-up from a portrait of President Washington, the U.S. seal, and the thirteen state seals of the United States of America, March 1, 1794, engraving, Amos Doolittle, Amos, Library of Congress Prints and Photographs Division. **Page 41**. Rendering of Wren Building at William and Mary College, painting, early 1900s, Library of Congress Prints and Photographs Division. **Page 44**. Skirmish at RICHMOND Jan. 5th 1781, map from Simcoe's military journal: a history of the operations of a partisan corps, called the Queen's Rangers, commanded by Lieut. Col. J.G. Simcoe, during the war of the American, John Graves Simcoe, LOC Rare Books. **Page 45**. *Thomas Jefferson*, painting, 1786, Mather Brown, National Portrait Gallery, Smithsonian Institution,

National Portrait Gallery, Smithsonian Institution/Art Resource, NY. **Page 48**. Martha 'Patsy' Jefferson Randolph, miniature watercolor or painting, 1789, Joseph Boze, the Diplomatic Reception Rooms, the U.S. Department of State. **Page 51**. Half Disme of 1792, obverse and reverse sides of silver coin, David Rittenhouse was then director of the mint. Reproduced with permission from the Robert H. Gore, Jr. Numismatic Collection, Department of Special Collections, University of Notre Dame Libraries. **Page 52**. Thomas Jefferson to Martha Jefferson, December 11, 1783, manuscript letter, Library of Congress Manuscript Division. **Page 54**. *Place de Greve*, painting, 1750, Nicolas Raguenet, and Jean Baptiste, Musee de la Ville de Paris, Musee Carnavalet, Paris, France / Bridgeman Art Library. **Page 55**. *Observations sur la Virginie*, title page, the title page date of 1786 was wrong, as the book was actually published in 1787, French edition of Thomas Jefferson's *Notes on the State of Virginia*, LOC Rare Books. **Page 56**. The Maison Carrée with the Amphitheatre and the Tour Magne at Nîmes, painting, 1786–1785, Hubert Robert, Louvre, Paris, France/Bridgeman Art Library. **Page 57**. Richmond, Virginia, Front view of Capitol, stereograph, 1865, Library of Congress Prints and Photographs Division. **Page 58**. Queen Marie Antoinette on the way to her execution, pen and ink, 1793, Jacques Louis David, Private Collection /Bridgeman Art Library. **Page 62**. *The First Cabinet*, engraving, 1857, engraved by T. Phillibrown after a painting by Alonzo Chappel, © Art Resource, NY. **Page 64**. *A Philosophic Cock*, aquatint, circa 1804, James Akin, Courtesy of the American Antiquarian Society, Worcester, Massachusetts, Picture History. **Page 65**. *A Peep into the Anti-Federal Club*, cartoon, 1793, Art Resource, NY. **Pages 68–69**. *Monticello*, watercolor, 1821, Jefferson Vail, © Réunion des Musées Nationaux / Art Resource, NY. **Page 72**. Jefferson's draft of "A Manual of Parliamentary Practice," manuscript, circa 1799–1801, Thomas Jefferson, Library of Congress Manuscript Division. **Page 74**. The Alien Act, July 6, 1798; Fifth Congress; Enrolled Acts and Resolutions; General Records of the United States Government; Record Group 11; National Archives, NARA. **Page 76**. Banner celebrating Jefferson's election victory in 1801, courtesy of NMAH Smithsonian Institution. **Page 78**. *A view of the Capitol of Washington before it was burnt down by the British*, circa 1800, watercolor, William Russell Birch, Library of Congress Prints and Photographs Division. **Page 79**. *Thomas Jefferson*, painting, circa 1801, Caleb Boyle, Kirby Collection of Historical Paintings, Lafayette College, Easton, Pennsylvania. **Page 82**. *A map exhibiting all the new discoveries in the interior parts of North America: inscribed by permission to the honourable governor and company of adventurers of England trading into Hudsons Bay in testimony of their liberal communications to their most obedient and very humble servant Aaron Arrowsmith, January 1st 1795*, map, published in London on Jan. 1, 1795 by A. Arrowsmith, No. 24 Rathbone Place, Library of Congress Geography and Map Division. (Note: Map adapted by addition of pink box.) **Page 84**. *Le General Bonaparte à Arcole, 17 Nov. 1796*, painting, Antoine Gros, circa 1796, © Erich Lessing / Art Resource, NY. **Page 89**. *View from the fort of New Orleans*, gouache, 1803, French school, © Réunion des Musées Nationaux / Art Resource, NY. **Page 93**. *Thomas Jefferson*, painting, 1805, Gilbert Stuart, National Portrait Gallery, Smithsonian Institution / Art Resource, NY. **Page 95**. *University of Virginia*, engraving, 1825, Peter Maverick, Courtesy of Monticello/Thomas Jefferson Foundation, Inc. **Page 97**. Thomas Jefferson's epitaph, not dated, Library of Congress Manuscript Division.

Credits

Photo Credits

Cover courtesy of Independence National Historical Park; cover (background), pp. 35, 74 National Archives and Records Administration; p. 4 The White House Collection, courtesy of the White House Historical Association; pp. 6, 20, 21, 90, 95 Courtesy of Monticello/Thomas Jefferson Foundation, Inc.; pp. 8, 82 Library of Congress Geography and Map Division; pp. 9, 26 Colonial Williamsburg Foundation; p. 11 Print and Picture Collection, the Free Library of Philadelphia; p. 13 Red Hill, The Patrick Henry National Memorial; p. 15 © Bibliotheque Nationale, Paris, France/Bridgeman Art Library; pp. 17, 18, 44, 55, Library of Congress Rare Book and Special Collections Division; pp. 24, 34, 39, 41, 57, 78, Library of Congress Prints and Photographs Division; pp. 29, 32, 52, 72, 97 Library of Congress Manuscript Division; p. 33 Frederick DeBourg Richards Photograph Collection at the Library Company of Philadelphia; p. 37 Library of Virginia; pp. 45, 93 National Portrait Gallery, Smithsonian Institution / Art Resource, NY; p. 50 the Diplomatic Reception Rooms, the United States Department of State; p. 51 reproduced with permission from the Robert H. Gore, Jr. Numismatic Collection, Department of Special Collections, University of Notre Dame Libraries; p. 54 © Musee de la Ville de Paris, Musee Carnavalet, Paris, France/Bridgeman Art Library; p. 56 © Louvre, Paris, France/Bridgeman Art Library; p. 58 © Private Collection/Bridgeman Art Library; pp. 62, 65 © Art Resource, NY; p. 64 Picture History; pp. 68–69, 89 © Réunion des Musées Nationaux / Art Resource, NY; p. 76 National Museum of American History, Smithsonian Institution; p. 79 Kirby Collection of Historical Paintings, Lafayette College, Easton, PA; p. 84 © Erich Lessing / Art Resource, NY; p. 98 © Scott T. Smith/CORBIS.

Project Editor

Daryl Heller

Series Design

Laura Murawski

Layout Design

Corinne L. Jacob

Ginny Chu

Photo Researcher

Jeffrey Wendt